HVAC SEO

How to Become the Top-Ranked HVAC Dealer in Your Area

Scott Orth

ISBN: 979-8-9897437-0-4

Table of Contents

SECTION 1:
IMPORTANCE OF SEO

Search Engine Optimization (SEO) is a critical aspect of digital marketing that focuses on optimizing websites and online content to enhance their visibility on search engine results pages (SERPs). The importance of SEO cannot be overstated in the context of online presence, visibility, and overall business success. Several vital factors highlight the significance of SEO:

1. **Increased Visibility and Traffic:** SEO helps improve a website's ranking on search engines, making it more likely to appear on the first page of search results. The higher a site ranks, the more visible it is to users, leading to increased organic (non-paid) traffic.

2. **Credibility and Trust:** Users often perceive websites at the top of search results as more trustworthy and credible. SEO helps build and establish the credibility of a website, contributing to a positive online reputation.

3. **User Experience Improvement:** SEO involves optimizing not only for search engines but also for a better user experience. This includes creating quality content, improving site structure and navigation, and ensuring fast loading times. A positive user experience can lead to higher engagement and satisfaction.

4. **Cost-Effectiveness:** SEO is a cost-effective strategy for driving organic traffic compared to paid advertising. While paid advertising can be beneficial, especially for short-term goals, SEO provides long-term sustainability without incurring ongoing costs for each click or impression.

5. **Targeted Audience Reach:** SEO allows businesses to target keywords and phrases relevant to their products or services. This helps reach a more targeted audience interested in the business's offers, increasing the likelihood of conversions.

6. **Adaptability to Market Changes:** Search engines frequently update their algorithms, and SEO strategies must adapt. Staying on top of SEO best practices ensures that a website remains relevant and performs well despite shifts in the online landscape.

7. **Competitive Advantage:** In today's competitive online landscape, businesses that invest in SEO gain a competitive edge. Outranking competitors in search results can capture a larger market share and attract potential customers before they discover alternatives.

8. **Insights into Customer Behavior:** SEO tools and analytics provide valuable insights into user behavior, preferences, and trends. By analyzing this data, businesses can make informed decisions, refine their strategies, and tailor their content to meet the needs of their target audience.

In conclusion, the importance of SEO lies in its ability to drive organic traffic, enhance online visibility, build credibility, and contribute to long-term business success in the digital age. A well-executed SEO strategy is fundamental to a comprehensive digital marketing plan.

CHAPTER 1:

INTRODUCTION TO THE SIGNIFICANCE OF ONLINE PRESENCE

In the rapidly evolving landscape of the digital era, establishing a robust online presence has become paramount for individuals, businesses, and organizations. An online presence encompasses the sum of a digital footprint, including websites, social media profiles, and various forms of online content. This presence is crucial for several reasons, as it reflects the essence of an entity and plays a pivotal role in shaping perceptions, fostering connections, and driving success in the virtual realm.

1. **Global Reach and Accessibility:** An online presence transcends geographical boundaries, providing the opportunity to connect with a global audience. Whether you are an entrepreneur, artist, or organization, the internet allows you to reach people worldwide, expanding your influence and potential impact.

2. **24/7 Availability:** Unlike physical storefronts or traditional modes of communication, the online realm operates around the clock. Establishing an online presence ensures constant accessibility for your audience, allowing them to engage with your content, products, or services anytime, fostering convenience and flexibility.

3. **Credibility and Trust Building:** A well-crafted online presence contributes to the credibility and trustworthiness of an individual or business. In the digital age, consumers often research online before making decisions, and a professional and consistent online presence can instill confidence, encouraging trust and loyalty.

4. **Brand Visibility and Recognition:** Building an online presence is synonymous with enhancing brand visibility. Through websites, social media platforms, and content marketing, entities can establish a recognizable brand identity, making it easier for their audience to identify and remember them amidst a sea of online offerings.

5. **Engagement and Interaction:** Online presence facilitates direct interaction and engagement with the audience. Social media channels, forums, and other online platforms provide real-time communication, feedback, and relationship-building opportunities, fostering community and connection.

6. **Market Expansion and Business Growth:** For businesses, a robust online presence opens avenues for market expansion and growth. E-commerce platforms enable sales beyond physical locations, and digital marketing strategies can target specific audiences, driving customer acquisition and revenue generation.

7. **Adaptability to Technological Trends:** The digital landscape is dynamic, with constant technological advancements. An online presence signifies an entity's adaptability to these changes, ensuring relevance and competitiveness in an environment where staying ahead of technological trends is crucial.

8. **Showcasing Expertise and Authority:** Individuals and businesses can use their online presence to showcase expertise and establish authority in their respective fields or niche markets. They can share knowledge, insights, and innovations through blogs, videos, and other content, positioning themselves as industry leaders.

In conclusion, the significance of online presence extends far beyond mere visibility; it is a dynamic tool that shapes perceptions, fosters connections, and drives success in an interconnected world. As we navigate the digital landscape, understanding and leveraging the power of online presence becomes an option and a strategic necessity for those seeking to thrive in the digital age.

UNDERSTANDING THE DIGITAL LANDSCAPE FOR HVAC BUSINESSES

In the modern business environment, the digital landscape plays a crucial role in the success and growth of companies across various industries, including heating, ventilation, and air conditioning (HVAC). As technology advances, consumers increasingly rely on digital platforms for information, services, and purchasing decisions. Here's an exploration of the critical aspects of the digital landscape for HVAC businesses:

1. **Online Presence and Website:** An HVAC business's online presence begins with a professional and user-friendly website. This is the digital storefront providing essential information about services, contact details, and customer testimonials. A well-optimized website improves visibility on search engines, making it easier for potential customers to find the business.

2. **Local SEO and Google My Business:** Local search engine optimization (SEO) is crucial for HVAC businesses, as many potential customers search for local services. Optimizing *Google My Business* profiles, including accurate business information, service areas, and customer reviews, enhances local visibility. This is especially important for attracting customers in need of immediate HVAC services.

3. **Content Marketing:** Content marketing is a powerful tool for HVAC businesses to showcase expertise and build trust. Creating relevant and valuable content, such as blog posts, articles, and video tutorials, can establish the business as an

industry authority. Content that addresses common HVAC issues, maintenance tips, and energy efficiency can resonate with the target audience.

4. **Social Media Engagement:** Social media platforms allow HVAC businesses to engage with their audience, share updates, and showcase their work. For this purpose, an entity can use online social media platforms like Facebook, Instagram, and LinkedIn to post before-and-after photos, customer testimonials, and promotions. Social media also allows for direct interaction with customers through comments and messages.

5. **Online Reviews and Reputation Management:** Positive online reviews influence the decision-making process for HVAC services. Encouraging satisfied customers to leave reviews on platforms like Google, Yelp, Trustpilot, and industry-specific websites can boost the business's reputation. Responding to positive and negative reviews demonstrates a commitment to customer satisfaction.

6. **Mobile Optimization:** Many consumers use mobile devices to search for HVAC services. Ensuring that websites are mobile-friendly is essential for providing a seamless experience to users on smartphones and tablets. Mobile optimization is also a factor that search engines consider when ranking websites.

7. **Pay-Per-Click (PPC) Advertising:** HVAC businesses can use PPC advertising to appear at the top of search engine results for specific keywords. This form of targeted advertising allows for precise control over the budget and geographic targeting, ensuring the business reaches potential customers in its service areas.

8. **Technological Integration:** Embracing technology in the HVAC industry is essential. This includes utilizing smart thermostats, energy-efficient systems, and other advancements. HVAC businesses highlighting their technical expertise and commitment to innovation will likely appeal to tech-savvy customers.

In conclusion, navigating the digital landscape is integral for HVAC businesses to stay competitive and connect with their target audience. From establishing a frequent online presence to leveraging local SEO, content marketing, and social media engagement, embracing digital strategies is vital to thriving in the dynamic and evolving HVAC industry.

EVOLUTION OF CONSUMER BEHAVIOR IN THE DIGITAL AGE

The evolution of consumer behavior in the digital age has been a dynamic and transformative journey driven by technological advancements, changing communication channels, and the widespread adoption of the internet. Understanding this evolution is crucial for businesses seeking to adapt and effectively engage with modern consumers. Here are the critical stages in the development of consumer behavior:

Early Internet Adoption:

- **1990s-2000s:** The initial phase saw the rise of internet adoption. Consumers started to explore the web for information, communication, and fundamental transactions. E-commerce emerged, allowing people to make online purchases, albeit with some skepticism.

Social Media and Interconnectivity:

- **The mid-2000s to Early 2010s:** The advent of social media platforms, such as Facebook, Twitter, and Instagram, transformed how consumers connect and share information. This era shifted towards peer influence and user-generated content, impacting purchasing decisions.

Mobile Revolution:

- **The mid-2010s:** The widespread use of smartphones brought a mobile-centric era. Consumers increasingly relied on mobile devices for browsing, social interaction, and shopping. Mobile apps and responsive websites have become imperative for businesses.

Rise of Online Reviews and Influencers:

- **Late 2010s:** Online reviews on platforms like Yelp and the influence of social media influencers gained prominence. Consumers began trusting peer reviews and influencer recommendations, impacting brand perception and purchase decisions.

Personalization and Data-driven Marketing:

- **Late 2010s to Present:** The digital age ushered in an era of personalized experiences. Businesses leverage data analytics and AI to tailor marketing messages, product recommendations, and user interfaces, enhancing customer engagement and satisfaction.

Ephemeral Content and Short-form Video:

- **Present:** The popularity of platforms like YouTube Shorts, Snapchat, TikTok, and Instagram Stories reflects a preference for short-form, engaging content. Consumers are drawn to authentic, real-time content that aligns with their fast-paced digital lifestyles.

E-commerce Dominance:

- **Present:** The COVID-19 pandemic accelerated the shift towards online shopping. E-commerce platforms, supported by secure payment gateways and convenient delivery options, became the primary retail mode for many consumers.

Concerns About Privacy and Security:

- **Present:** With increased data breaches and privacy concerns, consumers are more conscious about how their data is collected and used. Businesses must navigate the balance between personalization and respecting user privacy.

Social and Environmental Consciousness:

- **Present:** Modern consumers prioritize brands that align with their values, primarily social responsibility and environmental sustainability. Businesses are expected to demonstrate ethical practices and contribute positively to society.

Emergence of Voice Search and Smart Devices:

- **Present and Future:** The rise of voice-activated assistants and smart devices introduces new avenues for consumer interaction. Optimizing for voice search and adapting to the Internet of Things (IoT) becomes essential for businesses.

In summary, the evolution of consumer behavior in the digital age reflects a journey from fundamental internet adoption to a highly interconnected and data-driven landscape. Today's consumers are well-informed and empowered and seek personalized, ethical, and convenient experiences from the brands they engage with. Staying attuned to these evolving trends is crucial for businesses aiming to meet the expectations of the modern digital consumer.

EXPLORING THE CRITICAL ROLE OF SEARCH ENGINES IN CUSTOMER DECISION-MAKING

Search engines play a critical role in customer decision-making across various industries. As the gateway to information on the internet, search engines significantly influence how consumers discover, evaluate, and choose products or services. Here's an exploration of the essential role of search engines in shaping customer decisions:

Information Discovery:

- **Initiating the Decision-Making Process:** Search engines are the starting point for information-seeking consumers. Whether it's researching products, services, or solutions to a problem, customers often turn to search engines to discover relevant information.

Research and Comparison:

- **In-Depth Exploration:** Consumers conduct detailed research on search engines to compare options. They look for product features, reviews, prices, and other details that help them make informed decisions. SERPs provide a wealth of information that aids this comparative analysis.

Building Trust and Credibility:

- **Ranking and Reviews:** A website's position on search engine results conveys a sense of credibility to users. High-ranking websites are perceived as more informative and trustworthy. Additionally, reviews displayed in search results show transparency and contribute to building trust as consumers consider the experiences of others.

Local Searches and Decision-Making:

- **Local Business Impact:** For businesses with a physical presence, local searches on platforms like *Google My Business* influence customer decisions. Information such as business hours, location, and reviews help consumers decide which local businesses to engage with.

Mobile Search and Micro-Moments:

- **On-the-Go Decision-Making:** Mobile searches have become integral to decision-making in micro-moments, where consumers quickly turn to their smartphones for immediate needs. Whether looking for a nearby restaurant or comparing product prices, mobile search impacts real-time decision-making.

SEO and Brand Visibility:

- **Online Presence:** SEO enhances a brand's visibility on search engines. Businesses that invest in SEO are more likely to appear prominently in search results, increasing the chances of being considered by potential customers.

Paid Advertising and Promotions:

- **Strategic Marketing:** Paid advertising through search engine marketing (SEM) allows businesses to feature at the top of search results for specific keywords. This strategic placement increases visibility and influences customer decisions, especially for users ready to purchase.

Voice Search and Emerging Technologies:

- **Changing Search Dynamics:** The rise of voice search and integration of artificial intelligence (AI) in search engines introduce new dimensions to customer decision-making. Optimizing for voice queries becomes crucial as users seek more conversational and context-aware interactions.

Continuous Influence Throughout the Customer Journey:

- **Ongoing Engagement:** Search engines play a role in customer journey stages, from initial research to post-purchase reviews. They facilitate continuing engagement and interaction, shaping customer perceptions even after making a decision.

Adaptation to Evolving Consumer Behavior:

- **Dynamic Nature:** Search engines continuously adapt to changing consumer behavior and technological trends. Businesses must stay informed about these changes to adjust their strategies and maintain a strong online presence.

Search engines are pivotal in customer decision-making, influencing how consumers discover, evaluate, and ultimately choose products or services. Businesses that understand and strategically leverage the role of search engines can enhance their online visibility, build trust, and effectively connect with their target audience.

CHAPTER 2:

THE IMPACT OF SEO ON BRAND VISIBILITY AND CREDIBILITY

The impact of SEO on brand visibility and credibility is profound in the digital landscape. SEO strategies are designed to improve a website's ranking on SERPs, significantly affecting how a brand is perceived online. Here's an exploration of the essential ways in which SEO influences brand visibility and credibility:

Increased Online Visibility:

- **Higher Search Engine Rankings:** SEO aims to optimize a website's content, structure, and other elements to rank higher on SERPs. When a brand consistently appears at the top of relevant search results, it enjoys increased visibility among users actively searching for products or services.

Trust and Credibility Building:

- **Association with Authority:** High-ranking websites are often perceived as more credible and authoritative. When a brand consistently appears in top search results, it benefits from the implicit endorsement of search engines, contributing to trust-building among users.

Positive User Experience:

- **Site Optimization:** SEO involves optimizing website elements like speed, mobile responsiveness, and user-friendly navigation. A well-optimized site provides a positive user experience, reinforcing the brand's credibility in visitors' eyes.

Content Quality and Relevance:

- **Valuable Content:** SEO encourages the creation of high-quality and relevant content. Brands that produce informative, engaging, and useful content are favored by search algorithms and seen as knowledgeable authorities in their industry by users.

Local SEO and Business Trust:

- **Local Visibility:** For businesses with physical locations, local SEO is crucial. Local search results and positive reviews build trust among local consumers, who see the brand as a reputable option.

Reviews and Testimonials:

- **Visibility of Reviews:** SEO can influence the visibility of reviews in search results. Positive reviews displayed prominently contribute to the brand's credibility, assuring potential customers of the positive experiences of others.

Consistent Branding:

- **Branding Signals:** SEO involves optimizing elements, including meta tags, headers, and images. Consistent branding signals reinforce the brand's identity, making it easily recognizable and enhancing credibility over time.

Social Proof and Backlinks:

- **Backlink Building:** Quality backlinks, earned through reputable sources, are essential to SEO. When other authoritative websites link to a brand's content, it signals to search engines and users that the brand is a trusted and valuable resource.

Adaptation to User Intent:

- **User-Centric Approach:** SEO strategies focus on understanding and meeting user intent. Brands that align their content with what users are searching for demonstrate a commitment to addressing customer needs, contributing to credibility.

Competitive Advantage:

- **Outranking Competitors:** Brands that consistently invest in SEO gain a competitive edge. Outranking competitors in search results position the brand as a leader in the industry, attracting more attention and trust from potential customers.

In summary, the impact of SEO on brand visibility and credibility is multifaceted. It goes beyond achieving higher search rankings; it involves creating a positive user experience, offering valuable content, and building trust over time. As users increasingly rely on search engines to inform their decisions, brands prioritizing and investing in SEO stand to gain visibility, credibility, and long-term success in the digital landscape.

BUILDING A STRONG BRAND IMAGE THROUGH SEO

Building a strong brand image through SEO involves strategic planning and execution to enhance online visibility, credibility, and positive associations with your brand. Here's a comprehensive guide on how to leverage SEO to build a solid brand image:

Define Your Brand Identity:

- **Keywords Reflecting Brand Values:** Identify industry-friendly terms and phrases that reflect your brand's values, mission, and unique selling propositions. Use these keywords in your website content, meta tags, and other SEO elements.

Optimize Your Website:

- **User-Friendly Design:** Ensure your website is user-friendly, mobile-responsive, and offers a seamless experience. Fast loading times and intuitive navigation contribute to a positive user experience, reflecting well on your brand.

Create High-Quality Content:

- **Content Reflecting Brand Voice:** Develop content that aligns with your brand's voice, tone, and values. High-quality, informative, and engaging content attracts users and positions your brand as an authoritative resource in your industry.

Implement On-Page SEO Best Practices:

- **Optimized Meta Tags:** Craft compelling title tags, meta descriptions, and headers that incorporate your brand's key messages and keywords. These elements impact search rankings and influence users' perceptions of your brand.

Build a Strong Social Media Presence:

- **Integration with SEO Strategies:** Search engines take into account social signals like shares and likes on social media. Actively engage on social platforms, share your content, and encourage social sharing to enhance your brand's online presence.

Local SEO for Local Presence:

- **Optimize for Local Searches:** For brick-and-mortar businesses, optimize your website for local SEO. Claim and optimize your Google My Business listing, encourage customer reviews, and provide accurate location information to enhance local visibility.

Earn Quality Backlinks:

- **Link-Building Strategies:** Develop a link-building strategy to earn high-quality backlinks from reputable websites in your industry. Backlinks improve search rankings and contribute to your brand's perceived authority.

Focus on User Experience:

- **Site Usability and Accessibility:** Prioritize user experience by ensuring your website is accessible, easy to navigate, and provides valuable information. A positive user experience contributes to positive brand associations.

Monitor and Manage Online Reviews:

- **Responding to Reviews:** Actively monitor and respond to online reviews. Addressing positive and negative reviews demonstrates your commitment to customer satisfaction and can positively influence brand perception.

Mobile Optimization:

- **Responsive Design:** With the increasing use of mobile devices, ensure your website is enhanced for mobile users. Google considers mobile-friendliness a ranking factor, and a mobile-responsive site contributes to a positive user experience.

Utilize Structured Data Markup:

- **Enhanced Search Listings:** Implement structured data markup to provide search engines with additional information about your content. This can result in enhanced search listings, with features like rich snippets that make your brand stand out.

Consistent Branding Across Channels:

- **Uniform Branding Elements:** Maintain consistency in branding elements across all online channels. This includes your website, social media profiles, and other digital platforms. Consistency reinforces brand recognition and trust.

Stay Informed About SEO Trends:

- **Adaptation to Changes:** SEO is dynamic, and staying informed about industry trends and algorithm changes is crucial. Adapt your SEO strategy to align with evolving search engine requirements and user behaviors.

Promote Brand Values and CSR:

- **Highlighting Corporate Social Responsibility:** If applicable, showcase your brand's commitment to corporate social responsibility (CSR). This can be incorporated into content and outreach strategies, resonating with socially conscious consumers.

Track and Analyze Performance:

- **Data-Driven Decision-Making:** Use analytics tools to track the performance of your SEO efforts. Analyze user behavior, conversion rates, and other metrics to make data-driven decisions and continually improve your brand's online presence.

By combining these strategies, you can leverage SEO to improve your website's search engine rankings and shape a positive and compelling brand image. Consistent efforts in optimizing for visibility, user experience, and brand messaging contribute to a strong online presence and a favorable perception of your brand.

ENHANCING ONLINE CREDIBILITY AND TRUSTWORTHINESS

Enhancing online credibility and trustworthiness is crucial for building a positive reputation, establishing customer trust, and fostering long-term relationships. In the digital age, where consumers rely on online information to make decisions, businesses must enhance their online credibility. Here are strategies to achieve this:

Transparent and Honest Communication:

- Clearly communicate your business values, mission, and policies. Be transparent about your products or services, pricing, and potential limitations. Honest communication builds trust with your audience.

Consistent Branding:

- Maintain consistent branding across all online platforms, including your website, social media, and marketing materials. Consistency in visuals, messaging, and tone helps reinforce your brand identity and makes your business more trustworthy.

Professional Website Design:

- Invest in a professional and user-friendly website design. A well-designed website with intuitive navigation and high-quality content reflects positively on your business, instilling confidence in visitors.

Customer Reviews and Testimonials:

- Encourage satisfied customers to leave positive reviews and testimonials on your website and relevant review platforms. Displaying real experiences builds social proof and reassures potential customers of your reliability.

Secure Online Transactions:

- If your business involves online transactions, prioritize the security of customer information. Use secure payment gateways, display trust badges, and communicate your commitment to protecting customer data.

Quality Content Creation:

- Create high-quality and informative content that adds value to your audience. This can include blog posts, articles, videos, or infographics. Positioning your business as an authoritative source enhances credibility.

Social Media Engagement:

- Actively engage with your audience on social media platforms. Respond promptly to inquiries, address concerns, and participate in relevant conversations. Social media engagement humanizes your brand and builds trust.

Clear Contact Information:

- Ensure your contact information, including email addresses, phone numbers, and physical addresses, is easily accessible on your website. Providing clear and direct communication channels instills confidence.

Responsive Customer Support:

- Offer responsive and helpful customer support. Address inquiries and issues promptly and provide clear channels for customer assistance. A reliable customer support system contributes significantly to trustworthiness.

Secure and Accessible Website:

- Implement security measures to protect your website from cyber threats. Additionally, ensure your website is accessible to disabled users, showcasing a commitment to inclusivity.

Showcasing Industry Certifications:

- Prominently display industry certifications, awards, or affiliations on your website if applicable. These endorsements from authoritative sources add credibility to your business.

Clear Return and Refund Policies:

- Clearly outline your return and refund policies. Transparent policies demonstrate your commitment to customer satisfaction and reduce uncertainty, contributing to a positive perception of your business.

Community Engagement and CSR:

- Engage in community initiatives or corporate social responsibility (CSR) activities. Committing to social causes can enhance your brand's reputation and credibility.

Regularly Update And Maintain Content:

- Keep your website and other online channels up-to-date. Outdated information or broken links can undermine credibility. Regularly review and refresh your content to reflect current offerings and industry trends.

Monitor and Address Online Reputation:

- Actively monitor online mentions, reviews, and discussions about your brand. Address negative feedback professionally and proactively, showing your dedication to customer satisfaction.

You can enhance your credibility and trustworthiness by incorporating these strategies into your online presence and general business practices. Building a strong and trustworthy online image is an ongoing process that requires consistent effort and a commitment to delivering value and transparency to your audience.

CASE STUDIES: SUCCESSFUL HVAC BRANDS AND THEIR SEO JOURNEYS

Let's explore two potential scenarios:

Case Study 1: American Standard Heating and Air Conditioning

Background:

American Standard Heating and Air Conditioning (AS_HVAC) is a regional HVAC service provider focusing on residential and commercial heating and cooling solutions.

SEO Strategies:

1. **Local SEO Optimization:** AS_HVAC optimized its website for local search, including location-specific keywords in meta tags, headers, and content. They claimed and regularly updated their Google My Business profile, encouraging satisfied customers to leave positive reviews.

2. **Content Marketing:** The company invested in creating informative content related to HVAC maintenance, energy efficiency, and troubleshooting common issues. This content was shared on their website's blog, addressing customer queries and showcasing their expertise.

3. **Mobile Optimization:** Recognizing the importance of mobile users, AS_HVAC ensured that their website was mobile-friendly. This improved user experience and aligned with Google's mobile-first indexing, positively impacting search rankings.

4. **Technical SEO:** The company focused on technical aspects of SEO, including optimizing site speed, fixing crawl errors, and implementing schema markup. Search engines could easily understand and index their website's content.

5. **Link Building:** AS_HVAC engaged in ethical link-building practices, earning backlinks from local directories, industry associations, and reputable local businesses. These high-quality backlinks contributed to improved domain authority.

Results:

- **Improved Local Rankings:** AS_HVAC's focus on local SEO led to higher rankings in local search results, making them more visible to potential customers in their service areas.

- **Increased Website Traffic:** The combination of content marketing and technical SEO increased organic traffic to their website.

- **Enhanced Credibility:** Positive online reviews and informative content have established AS_HVAC as a trustworthy and knowledgeable HVAC service provider.

Case Study 2: Allied Commercial

Background:

Allied Commercial is a national HVAC equipment manufacturer and distributor.

SEO Strategies:

1. **Keyword Optimization:** Allied Commercial conducted thorough keyword research to identify industry-specific and product-related keywords. These keywords were strategically incorporated into product descriptions, meta tags, and page content.

2. **E-commerce SEO:** Recognizing the importance of online sales, the company implemented e-commerce SEO strategies, optimizing product pages, utilizing schema markup for product details, and ensuring a seamless online purchasing process.

3. **Rich Snippets and Structured Data:** Allied Commercial utilized rich snippets and structured data to enhance the appearance of their product listings in search results. This included displaying product prices, availability, and ratings directly in the search snippet.

4. **Technical SEO for Large Websites:** Managing a large e-commerce website, Allied Commercial implemented technical SEO practices for site architecture, including XML sitemaps, breadcrumb navigation, and effective categorization of products.

5. **International SEO:** Given its national presence, Allied Commercial implemented international SEO strategies for specific product lines, catering to regional preferences and search patterns.

Results:

- **Increased Online Sales:** E-commerce SEO efforts improved visibility and rankings, growing online sales for HVAC equipment.

- **Enhanced User Experience:** Technical SEO improvements and a user-friendly e-commerce platform resulted in a positive online experience for customers.

- **Global Visibility:** International SEO strategies enabled Company B to reach a broader audience, catering to different regional markets.

In both case studies, the success of the HVAC brands in their SEO journeys was influenced by a combination of local or national optimization, content marketing, technical SEO, and a focus on user experience. Collectively, these strategies contributed to improved visibility, credibility, and business growth. Remember that real-world scenarios can vary, and successful SEO requires ongoing adaptation to industry trends and algorithm changes.

CHAPTER 3:

UNDERSTANDING CUSTOMER BEHAVIOR AND THE ROLE OF SEARCH ENGINES

Understanding customer behavior and the role of search engines is crucial for businesses looking to effectively reach and engage their target audience in the digital landscape. Here's an exploration of the critical aspects of customer behavior and the significant role that search engines play in shaping these behaviors:

Information Discovery:

- **Customer Behavior:** Customers often start their journey by seeking information. This could be related to solving a problem, making a purchase decision, or simply satisfying curiosity.

- **Role of Search Engines:** Search engines serve as the primary tool for information discovery. Users input queries to find relevant and reliable information, making search engines the gateway to vast online content.

Research and Consideration:

- **Customer Behavior:** After discovering information, customers engage in research and consideration. They compare options, read reviews, and seek additional details to make informed decisions.

- **Role of Search Engines:** Search engines facilitate the research phase by providing diverse sources. Customers rely on search results to find product reviews, expert opinions, and comprehensive information on available options.

Online Shopping Behavior:

- **Customer Behavior:** Many consumers now prefer online shopping. They research products online, compare prices, and read reviews before purchasing.

- **Role of Search Engines:** Search engines are central to online shopping. Users often start with product searches, and search engine results guide them to e-commerce platforms, product pages, and reviews.

Local Searches and Physical Visits:

- **Customer Behavior:** Local searches are common for customers looking for nearby businesses, services, or products. Customers may use search engines to find directions, hours of operation, or contact information.

- **Role of Search Engines:** Local SEO and map features on search engines contribute to customers' ability to find and engage with businesses nearby. Google My Business listings, for example, are crucial for local visibility.

Mobile Search Behavior:

- **Customer Behavior:** With the prevalence of smartphones, customers frequently engage in mobile searches. They seek quick answers, location-based information, and on-the-go solutions.

- **Role of Search Engines:** Search engines prioritize mobile-friendly websites and provide location-based results, aligning with users' preferences for quick and accessible information.

Voice Search Adoption:

- **Customer Behavior:** The rise of voice-activated devices has increased voice searches. Customers now use voice commands for searches, especially when using smart speakers or mobile devices.

- **Role of Search Engines:** Search engines adapt to voice search trends by refining algorithms to understand conversational queries. Businesses need to optimize for voice search to remain relevant.

Brand Discovery and Recognition:

- **Customer Behavior:** Customers often discover new brands through online channels. Consistent branding and positive online presence contribute to brand recognition and recall.

- **Role of Search Engines:** Search engines influence brand discovery through organic search results and paid advertising. Brands that appear prominently in search results gain visibility and recognition.

Influence of Search Engine Rankings:

- **Customer Behavior:** Users trust and click on results at the top of search engine rankings. They associate higher rankings with credibility and relevance.

- **Role of Search Engines:** Search engine algorithms assess factors like relevance, authority, and user experience to determine rankings. Businesses strive to optimize their online presence to secure higher positions in search results.

Feedback and Reviews:

- **Customer Behavior:** Customers actively seek feedback and reviews from other users before making decisions. They trust the opinions and experiences shared by peers.

- **Role of Search Engines:** Search engines display reviews directly in search results. Businesses must manage online reviews as they significantly influence customer perceptions and decisions.

Continuous Learning and Adaptation:

- **Customer Behavior:** Customers are adaptive and continuously learning about new technologies, products, and trends. They expect businesses to keep up with their evolving needs.

- **Role of Search Engines:** Search engines evolve to match changing user behaviors. Businesses must stay informed about search engine updates, algorithms, and emerging technologies to effectively reach and engage their audience.

In summary, customer behavior and search engines are interconnected elements in the digital landscape. Businesses that understand and adapt to how customers use search engines can strategically position themselves to meet customer needs, enhance visibility, and build lasting relationships. The role of search engines is dynamic, and businesses need to stay agile to leverage these platforms effectively.

ANALYZING CUSTOMER SEARCH PATTERNS IN THE HVAC INDUSTRY

Analyzing customer search patterns in the HVAC (Heating, Ventilation, and Air Conditioning) industry is crucial for businesses to understand how potential customers seek information and make decisions. Here's an exploration of common customer search patterns in the HVAC industry:

Seasonal Variations:

- **Search Behavior:** Customer search patterns often exhibit seasonality. During colder months, users may search for heating-related services, such as furnace maintenance or repair. In warmer months, searches may shift towards air conditioning services.

Problem-Solving Queries:

- **Search Behavior:** Customers frequently use search engines to find solutions to specific HVAC problems. Queries may include issues like "no heat in the furnace," "AC not cooling," or "strange HVAC noises."

- **Content Focus:** HVAC businesses can create content that addresses common problems, offering troubleshooting guides, tips, and when to seek professional help.

Energy Efficiency and Savings:

- **Search Behavior:** Users are increasingly interested in energy-efficient HVAC solutions. They may search for terms like "energy-efficient HVAC systems," "smart thermostats," or "HVAC rebate programs."

- **Content Focus:** HVAC businesses can create content highlighting the energy efficiency of their products and services, including information on available incentives.

Product Research and Reviews:

- **Search Behavior:** Customers often research HVAC products before making a purchase. Queries might include "best HVAC brands," "top-rated furnaces," or "HVAC system reviews."

- **Content Focus:** HVAC businesses can create content comparing different products, providing reviews, and showcasing the benefits of their offerings.

Local Searches for Services:

- **Search Behavior:** When needing HVAC services, users often perform local searches. This includes queries like "HVAC repair near me," "AC installation [city]," or "emergency heating services."

- **Local SEO Focus:** HVAC businesses should prioritize local search engine optimization (SEO) to ensure visibility in local search results.

DIY Maintenance and Tips:

- **Search Behavior:** Customers may search for DIY HVAC maintenance tips or guides. Common queries include "how to clean AC filters," "DIY furnace troubleshooting," or "HVAC maintenance checklist."

- **Content Focus:** HVAC businesses can create educational content providing step-by-step guides for basic maintenance tasks. Emphasize when professional help is needed.

Cost-related Inquiries:

- **Search Behavior:** Users often search for cost-related information, such as "average HVAC repair costs," "cost to replace HVAC system," or "HVAC financing options."

- **Content Focus:** HVAC businesses can create content explaining cost factors, offering transparent pricing information, and providing financing options.

Comparisons and Upgrades:

- **Search Behavior:** Customers considering system upgrades or replacements may search for comparisons. Queries might include "central AC vs. ductless mini-split," "HVAC system upgrade benefits," or "latest HVAC technologies."

- **Content Focus:** HVAC businesses can create content comparing different systems, outlining the advantages of upgrades, and showcasing cutting-edge technologies.

HVAC Maintenance Plans:

- **Search Behavior:** Users interested in proactive HVAC care may search for "HVAC maintenance plans," "benefits of regular HVAC maintenance," or "annual HVAC service contracts."

- **Content Focus:** HVAC businesses can highlight the importance of regular maintenance, offer service plans, and explain the long-term benefits for customers.

Emergency Situations:

- **Search Behavior:** During emergencies, customers seek immediate assistance. Queries might include "24/7 HVAC emergency service," "urgent furnace repair," or "AC breakdown help."

- **Responsive Online Presence:** HVAC businesses should ensure their online presence is optimized for emergency queries, including clear contact information and a rapid response system.

Analyzing and understanding these search patterns allows HVAC businesses to tailor their online presence, content strategies, and services to meet the specific needs of potential customers. By addressing customers' diverse queries and concerns through search engines, HVAC businesses can enhance their visibility, credibility, and overall customer satisfaction.

THE CUSTOMER'S JOURNEY: FROM SEARCH TO CONVERSION

The customer's journey from search to conversion is a multi-stage process involving various touchpoints and business interactions. Understanding this journey is crucial for businesses to effectively engage with customers at each stage and optimize their marketing strategies. Here's a breakdown of the typical phases in the customer's journey:

Awareness Stage:

- **Search Behavior:** Customers initiate their journey by identifying a need or a problem. They use search engines to explore and gather information about potential solutions. Queries may be broad and informational.

- **Marketing Strategy:** Businesses can create awareness through content marketing, SEO, and paid advertising that addresses customer pain points and introduces their products or services as potential solutions.

Consideration Stage:

- **Search Behavior:** Customers narrow down their options and start comparing different solutions. They may use more specific queries like product comparisons, reviews, or feature-specific searches.

- **Marketing Strategy:** Businesses should provide detailed information, comparisons, and reviews through content. Remarketing campaigns can remind customers of the solutions they've explored.

Decision Stage:

- **Search Behavior:** Customers are ready to decide and may search for specific brands, models, or local providers. They might look for pricing information, special offers, or customer testimonials.

- **Marketing Strategy:** Businesses must be visible in branded searches and provide straightforward, persuasive content. Offering promotions or discounts can be effective in influencing the decision.

Conversion Stage:

- **Search Behavior:** Customers take a direct action, such as purchasing, filling out a contact form, or calling for a service. This stage may involve transactional searches like "buy [product]" or "schedule HVAC service."

- **Marketing Strategy:** Ensure a seamless online experience, optimize conversion paths, and provide clear calls to action. Post-conversion, thank-you pages, and follow-up communication are essential.

Post-Purchase Engagement:

- **Search Behavior:** Customers may continue engaging with the business after conversion. They might search for order tracking, product usage tips, or post-purchase support.

- **Marketing Strategy:** Implement post-purchase engagement strategies, such as personalized email campaigns, customer loyalty programs, and targeted content addressing common post-purchase questions.

Retention and Advocacy:

- **Search Behavior:** Satisfied customers may become advocates and recommend the brand to others. They may share positive experiences through reviews, testimonials, or social media.

- **Marketing Strategy:** Encourage and incentivize customer advocacy. Maintain communication through newsletters, exclusive offers, and loyalty programs. Monitor and respond to online reviews to nurture a positive reputation.

Re-engagement and Upselling:

- **Search Behavior:** For businesses offering repeatable or upgradable products/services, customers may search for new features, upgrades, or re-purchase considerations.

- **Marketing Strategy:** Implement re-engagement campaigns through targeted ads, email newsletters, and personalized recommendations. Highlight the benefits of upgrades or complementary products.

Feedback and Improvement:

- **Search Behavior:** Customers may express feedback or concerns through online searches, such as "product/service reviews" and "how to improve [product/service]."

- **Marketing Strategy:** Actively seek and respond to customer feedback. Use insights you have gained from search behavior and reviews to improve and enhance products or services.

Understanding the customer's journey from search to conversion involves a holistic approach, integrating various marketing channels and strategies tailored to each stage. Businesses that effectively align their marketing efforts with the customer's journey can build strong relationships, enhance customer satisfaction, and drive long-term success. Regular analysis and adaptation based on customer behavior and feedback are vital to refining this journey.

UTILIZING SEO TO ALIGN WITH CUSTOMER NEEDS AND EXPECTATIONS

Aligning SEO with customer needs and expectations is essential for businesses to create a user-focused online presence that attracts visitors and provides a positive experience. Here are strategies to utilize SEO effectively in meeting customer needs:

Comprehensive Keyword Research:

- **Understanding Customer Intent:** Conduct thorough keyword research to identify customers' terms and phrases when searching for products or services. Focus on keywords that align with user intent and reflect their needs.

Content Optimization:

- **Addressing Customer Questions:** Optimize website content to address customer queries and concerns. Create valuable, informative, and well-structured content that directly addresses the needs of your target audience.

User-Centric Website Design:

- **Optimizing for User Experience:** Ensure your website is user-friendly and easy to navigate. A well-designed website that caters to user needs contributes to higher engagement and improved search rankings.

Local SEO for Local Customer Base:

- **Targeting Local Keywords:** If your business serves a local audience, optimize for local SEO. Use location-specific keywords, claim and optimize your Google My Business listing, and encourage local customer reviews.

Mobile Optimization:

- **Catering to Mobile Users:** Given the prevalence of mobile searches, optimize your website for mobile devices. A responsive design ensures a positive experience for users on smartphones and tablets.

Featured Snippets and Quick Answers:

- **Providing Quick Solutions:** Structure content to be eligible for featured snippets. Offering quick and concise answers to common customer queries enhances visibility and aligns with the expectation of immediate information.

Voice Search Optimization:

- **Adapting to Voice Queries:** Optimize content for voice search as more users rely on voice-activated devices. Consider the conversational nature of voice searches and provide content that answers natural language queries.

Customer-Centric Meta Tags:

- **Clear and Compelling Titles/Descriptions:** Create compelling title tags and meta descriptions that accurately represent the content. These elements are crucial in enticing users to click on your search results.

Local Business Information:

- **Ensuring Accuracy:** For local businesses, ensure that your contact information, business hours, and location details are accurate and consistent across online platforms. This information directly serves customer expectations when they are searching for local services.

Customer Reviews and Testimonials:

- **Showcasing Positive Experiences:** Encourage and showcase customer reviews and testimonials on your website. Positive reviews build trust and directly address the expectations of potential customers.

Technical SEO for Accessibility:

- **Ensuring Accessibility:** Implement technical SEO practices to improve website accessibility. This includes optimizing page speed, fixing crawl errors, and ensuring compatibility with assistive technologies for disabled users.

E-A-T (Expertise, Authoritativeness, Trustworthiness):

- **Building Trust:** Establish your expertise in your industry. Create authoritative content, showcase credentials, and demonstrate trustworthiness to align with customer expectations for reliable information.

Consistent Brand Messaging:

- **Uniformity Across Channels:** Maintain consistent messaging and branding across all online channels. This creates a cohesive and recognizable brand image that aligns with customer expectations.

Regular Monitoring and Adaptation:

- **Staying Informed:** Regularly monitor changes in customer behavior and search trends. Adapt your SEO strategy to align with evolving customer needs and search engine algorithms.

Data Analysis for Continuous Improvement:

- **Iterative Approach:** Utilize analytics tools to analyze user behavior, search patterns, and website performance. Use data-driven insights to improve your SEO strategy and better meet customer expectations iteratively.

By incorporating these strategies, businesses can leverage SEO to enhance visibility and rankings and align with their target audience's needs and expectations. A customer-centric approach to SEO improves user satisfaction, increases trust, and, ultimately, improves business outcomes.

SECTION 2:

A-Z SEO GUIDE FOR HVAC DEALERS

Below is an A-Z SEO guide tailored for HVAC dealers. This guide covers key search engine optimization (SEO) aspects to help HVAC dealers improve their online visibility and attract more customers.

A - Audit Your Website

- **Accessibility:** Ensure your website is accessible to search engines and users. Use tools like Google Search Console to identify and fix accessibility issues.

B - Blogging

- **Content Strategy:** Develop a blog with informative content related to HVAC systems, energy efficiency, maintenance tips, etc. Regularly update it to keep the content fresh.

C - Content Optimization

- **Keywords:** Research and use relevant keywords in your content. Focus on long-tail keywords specific to HVAC services in your area.

D - Directory Listings

- **Local Directories:** List your business on local directories like Google My Business, Yelp, and other relevant platforms.

E - Engaging Content

- **Video Content:** Create engaging content about HVAC services, installations, and maintenance. Host videos on platforms like YouTube and embed them on your site.

F - Fast Loading

- **Website Speed:** Optimize your website for speed. Users and search engines prefer fast-loading sites.

G – Google Business Profile (formerly Google My Business)

- **GBP Optimization:** Optimize your Google Business Profile (GBP) with accurate business information, including location, contact details, and business hours.

H - High-Quality Backlinks

- **Backlink Building:** Build high-quality backlinks from reputable websites related to home improvement, local businesses, and industry publications.

I - Image Optimization

- **Alt Text:** Include descriptive alt text for images to improve accessibility and provide context for search engines.

J - JSON-LD Markup

- **Structured Data:** Implement JSON-LD markup to provide search engines with structured information about your business, services, and reviews.

K - Keep Track

- **Analytics:** Use tools like Google Analytics to track website performance, user behavior, and the effectiveness of your SEO efforts.

L - Local SEO

- **Local Keywords:** Target local keywords to enhance your visibility in local search results.

M - Mobile Optimization

- **Mobile-Friendly Design:** Ensure your website is mobile-friendly. Google prioritizes mobile-first indexing.

N - NAP Consistency

- **Name, Address, Phone:** Maintain consistent NAP (Name, Address, Phone) information across all online platforms.

O - On-Page SEO

- **Title Tags and Meta Descriptions:** Optimize each page's title tags and meta descriptions with relevant keywords.

P - Page Speed

- **Optimize Images:** Compress and use efficient formats to improve page load times.

Q - Quality Content

- **Informative Content:** Focus on creating high-quality, informative content that addresses the needs and concerns of your target audience.

R - Responsive Design

- **Responsive Website:** Ensure your website design is responsive to different screen sizes and devices.

S - Social Media Presence

- **Social Signals:** Maintain an active presence on social media platforms. Social signals can indirectly impact search rankings.

T - Technical SEO

- **Crawl Errors:** Regularly check for crawl errors, fix broken links, and ensure proper site indexing.

U - User Experience

- **User-Friendly Design:** Enhance user experience with an intuitive website design and easy navigation.

V - Voice Search Optimization

- **Voice-Friendly Content:** Optimize content for voice search by focusing on natural language and conversational keywords.

W - Website Security

- **SSL Certificate:** Secure your website with an SSL certificate. Google gives preference to secure sites.

X - XML Sitemap

- **Sitemap Submission:** Submit your XML sitemap to search engines to help them understand the structure of your website.

Y - Yelp and Other Review Platforms

- **Customer Reviews:** Encourage satisfied customers to leave reviews on platforms like Yelp. Respond to both positive and negative reviews professionally.

Z - Zero in on Local Keywords

- **Localized Keywords:** Emphasize keywords specific to your service area to target local customers effectively.

Implementing these strategies will contribute to a comprehensive and effective SEO plan for HVAC dealers, enhancing online visibility and attracting potential customers. Remember that SEO is an ongoing process; regularly updating and refining your strategies is crucial for long-term success.

CHAPTER 4:

KEYWORD RESEARCH SPECIFIC TO HVAC INDUSTRY

Conducting keyword research specific to the HVAC (Heating, Ventilation, and Air Conditioning) industry is essential for creating an effective SEO strategy. By identifying relevant keywords, you can optimize your website's content to match the terms your target audience uses in search engines. Here's a guide on conducting keyword research for the HVAC industry:

Understand Your Business:

- **Services and Products:** List all the services and products your HVAC business offers, including installation, repair, maintenance, and specific types of HVAC systems or equipment.

Identify Seed Keywords:

- **Industry Terms:** Start with broad industry terms like "HVAC," "heating services," "air conditioning repair," and "ventilation systems." These are your seed keywords.

Localize Keywords:

- **Location-specific Terms:** Incorporate location-specific keywords to target your local audience. For example, "HVAC services in [Your City]."

Long-Tail Keywords:

- **Specific Queries:** Include long-tail keywords that reflect specific queries users might have, such as "how to maintain a furnace," "best air conditioning brands," or "energy-efficient heating solutions."

Competitor Analysis:

- **Competitor Keywords:** Analyze the websites of competitors in the HVAC industry. Identify keywords they are targeting and performing well for.

Use Keyword Research Tools:

- **Google Keyword Planner:** Utilize Google Keyword Planner to find search volumes, competition, and related keywords. Input your seed keywords to generate additional ideas.

- **SEMrush or Ahrefs:** These tools provide insights into competitors' keywords, organic search traffic, and backlink profiles. Use them to identify gaps in your keyword strategy.

Seasonal Keywords:

- **Weather-Related Terms:** Given the seasonal nature of HVAC services, include keywords related to weather conditions, such as "winter HVAC maintenance," "summer AC installation," or "fall furnace repair."

FAQs and Customer Inquiries:

- **Customer Questions:** Consider the questions customers frequently ask. Create content around these queries and use them as keywords. For instance, "How often should I service my HVAC system?"

Brand-Specific Keywords:

- **Your Brand Terms:** Include keywords related to your brand name and variations. This is crucial for brand visibility and attracting customers looking for your services.

User Intent:

- **Searcher Intent:** Understand the intent behind specific keywords. Some users may seek information (informational purpose), while others might be ready to purchase (transactional plan).

Filter and Prioritize Keywords:

- **Relevance and Volume:** Filter your list based on relevance and search volume. Prioritize keywords that align with your business goals and have a decent search volume.

Create Content Around Keywords:

- **Content Strategy:** Develop a content strategy based on the identified keywords. Create blog posts, service pages, and FAQs that incorporate these keywords naturally.

Monitor and Adjust:

- **Regular Review:** Periodically review the performance of your chosen keywords using analytics tools. Adjust your strategy based on changes in search trends or business focus.

Localized Keywords for SEO:

- **Local Search Terms:** Emphasize local SEO by incorporating keywords that include your city or service areas. This is crucial for attracting local customers.

Following these steps, you'll develop a robust list of keywords tailored to the HVAC industry, helping you optimize your website, improve search engine rankings, and attract the right audience. Regularly update your keyword strategy to stay relevant in this dynamic industry.

IMPORTANCE OF TARGETED KEYWORDS FOR HVAC BUSINESSES

Targeted keywords play a crucial role in the success of online HVAC (Heating, Ventilation, and Air Conditioning) businesses. Here are several reasons highlighting the importance of targeted keywords for HVAC businesses:

Relevance to Services:

- **Alignment with Offerings:** Targeted keywords ensure that your online content is directly relevant to your HVAC business's services and products. This relevance enhances the chances of attracting the right audience interested in HVAC solutions.

Improved Search Engine Rankings:

- **Visibility in Search Results:** By optimizing your website for targeted keywords, you increase the likelihood of ranking higher in search engine results pages (SERPs). This improved visibility helps potential customers find your HVAC business when searching for related services.

Targeting Local Customers:

- **Local SEO Benefits:** Including location-specific keywords helps HVAC businesses target local customers. This is particularly important for location-dependent services, as customers often include their location when searching for HVAC providers.

Better Click-Through Rates (CTRs):

- **Relevance and Clickability:** When your website appears in search results for queries closely related to your services, users are likelier to click on your link. Targeted keywords increase the click-through rates, driving more organic traffic to your website.

Cost-Effective Advertising:

- **Pay-Per-Click (PPC) Efficiency:** In paid advertising campaigns, targeting keywords ensures that your ads are shown to users actively searching for HVAC services. This targeted approach maximizes your PPC campaign's efficiency, potentially reducing advertising costs.

Addressing Customer Intent:

- **Meeting User Needs:** Targeted keywords help you understand customer intent. Whether users seek information, seek services, or are ready to purchase, aligning with their goal through keywords enhances user satisfaction.

Content Relevance and Quality:

- **High-Quality Content:** Targeted keywords guide the creation of high-quality, informative content. This content not only addresses user queries but also positions your HVAC business as an authority in the industry.

Competitive Advantage:

- **Outranking Competitors:** Using targeted keywords effectively can help your HVAC business outrank competitors in search results. This is particularly important in competitive markets where companies vie for the attention of potential customers.

Seasonal and Trend-Related Optimization:

- **Adaptation to Trends:** Targeted keywords allow HVAC businesses to optimize their online presence based on seasonal trends and industry developments. For instance, altering keywords seasonally to address heating or cooling needs.

Better Conversion Rates:

- **Attracting Qualified Leads:** Users who find your website through targeted keywords are likelier to be interested in your HVAC services. This increases the likelihood of converting website visitors into actual customers.

Monitoring and Adjusting Strategy:

- **Data-Driven Optimization:** Tracking the performance of targeted keywords provides valuable data. This data can be used to refine your SEO strategy, identify which keywords are most effective, and adapt your approach accordingly.

Voice Search Adaptation:

- **Voice Search Compatibility:** As voice search becomes more prevalent, targeted keywords help HVAC businesses adapt their content to align with the conversational nature of voice queries.

In summary, targeted keywords are the foundation of a successful online presence for HVAC businesses. They contribute to improved visibility, higher search engine rankings, and increased relevance to potential customers. As the digital landscape evolves, staying vigilant in keyword research and optimization is essential for maintaining a competitive edge in the HVAC industry.

TOOLS AND TECHNIQUES FOR EFFECTIVE KEYWORD RESEARCH

Effective keyword research is vital for developing a successful SEO strategy. Here are various tools and techniques you can use for thorough and effective keyword research:

Tools for Keyword Research:

Google Keyword Planner:

- **Purpose:** Ideal for discovering new keywords and estimating search volumes.

- **Features:**
  - Provides historical search volume data;suggests new keywords based on a seed keyword, andoffers insights into the competition level for each keyword.

SEMrush:

- **Purpose:** Comprehensive SEO tool for competitive analysis and keyword research.

- **Features:**
  - Identifies organic and paid competitors;offers keyword difficulty scores, andprovides data on CPC (Cost Per Click) and search volume.

Ahrefs:

- **Purpose:** A powerful tool for backlink analysis and keyword research.

- **Features:**
  - Offerskeywordexplorerforfindingnewkeywords;provides data on search volume, keyword difficulty, and CPC, and helps identify content gaps and opportunities.

Moz Keyword Explorer:

- **Purpose:** Focuses on providing actionable insights for keyword research.

- **Features:**
    - Offers keyword suggestions with priority scores; provides insights into SERP features and gives an overview of the ranking potential.

Ubersuggest:

- **Purpose:** A free tool for keyword ideas and basic SEO metrics.
- **Features:**
    - Provides keyword suggestions and content ideas;offers data on search volume, CPC, and competition, and shows historical keyword performance.

AnswerThePublic:

- **Purpose:** Great for understanding questions users ask related to a topic.
- **Features:**
    - Presents visual representations of questions users ask around a keyword.
    - Helpful in creating content that addresses user queries.

Google Trends:

- **Purpose:** Helps understand the popularity of a keyword over time.
- **Features:**
    - Provides insights into search trends.
    - Allows comparison of the popularity of multiple keywords.

Techniques for Keyword Research:

Brainstorming:

- **Method:** Start by brainstorming a list of seed keywords related to your business.

- **Tip:** Consider your products, services, industry terms, and customer queries.

Competitor Analysis:

- **Method:** Analyze the keywords your competitors are targeting.

- **Tip:** Use tools like SEMrush or Ahrefs to identify competitor keywords and evaluate their performance.

Long-Tail Keywords:

- Method: Look for specific, longer phrases that users might search for.

- Tip: Long-tail keywords often have lower competition and can be more targeted.

Location-Based Keywords:

- **Method:** Include location-specific keywords if your business serves a local audience.

- **Tip:** Use city names, neighborhoods, or regional terms in your keywords.

Semantic Keywords:

- **Method:** Identify related terms and synonyms for your main keywords.

- **Tip:** This helps capture a broader range of search queries.

User Surveys and Feedback:

- **Method:** Collect input from customers or site visitors.

- **Tip:** Use surveys or feedback forms to understand your audience's language.

Content Gap Analysis:

- Method: Identify topics or keywords your competitors are ranking for that you aren't.

- Tip: Create content to fill these gaps and attract a similar audience.

Seasonal and Trend-Based Keywords:

- **Method:** Consider the seasonality of your business and industry trends.

- **Tip:** Adjust your keyword strategy to align with seasonal demands and emerging trends.

Regularly review and update your keyword strategy as industry trends, search algorithms, and user behavior evolve. A combination of tools and techniques will provide a comprehensive approach to effective keyword research.

BUILDING A COMPREHENSIVE HVAC KEYWORD STRATEGY

Building a comprehensive HVAC keyword strategy is crucial for optimizing your online presence and attracting the right audience. Here's a step-by-step guide to help you develop an effective keyword strategy for your HVAC business:

Understand Your HVAC Business:

- **Services and Specializations:** Clearly define the HVAC services you offer, including installation, repair, maintenance, and any specialized services.

- **Target Audience:** Identify your target audience, including residential or commercial clients and specific geographic areas you serve.

Conduct Initial Keyword Brainstorming:

- **List Seed Keywords:** Brainstorm a list of seed keywords related to your HVAC business. Include general terms like "HVAC," "heating services," and "air conditioning repair."

Competitor Analysis:

- **Identify Competitors:** Analyze competitors in your industry. Identify keywords they are ranking for and their overall online strategy.

- **Competitor Tools:** Use tools like SEMrush or Ahrefs to analyze competitor keywords, backlinks, and content strategies.

Localize Your Keywords:

- **Location-Specific Terms:** Include location-specific keywords if your HVAC business serves a specific location. For example, "HVAC services in [Your City]."

Long-Tail Keywords:

- **Specific Queries:** Incorporate long-tail keywords that reflect users' queries, such as "furnace maintenance tips" or "energy-efficient HVAC upgrades."

Seasonal and Trend-Based Keywords:

- **Weather-Related Terms:** Given the seasonal nature of HVAC services, include keywords related to weather conditions, such as "summer AC maintenance" or "winter heating solutions."

Semantic Keywords:

- **Related Terms:** Identify synonyms and associated terms for your main keywords. This helps capture a broader range of search queries.

Focus on User Intent:

- **Understand Intent:** Consider the intent behind user searches. Some users may seek information, while others are ready to schedule a service. Tailor your keywords accordingly.

Keyword Tools and Data Analysis:

- **Google Keyword Planner:** Use Google Keyword Planner to find search volumes, competition levels, and additional keyword ideas.

- **SEMrush or Ahrefs:** Leverage these tools for in-depth keyword analysis, competitive insights, and identifying gaps in your strategy.

Create a Comprehensive Keyword List:

- **Categorize Keywords:** Organize your keywords into categories based on services, location, and user intent.

- **Prioritize Keywords:** Prioritize keywords based on relevance, search volume, and competition.

Content Mapping:

- **Assign Keywords to Content:** Map keywords to specific pages on your website. Ensure each page is [1]augmented for a set of related keywords.

- **Create Content:** Develop high-quality content that aligns with targeted keywords. This includes service pages, blog posts, and FAQs.

Optimize On-Page Elements:

- **Title Tags and Meta Descriptions:** Craft compelling title tags and meta descriptions with targeted keywords.

- **Header Tags:** Use header tags (H1, H2, H3) to structure content and include relevant keywords.

- **URL Structure:** Optimize URLs to include key terms.

---

1 Return On Investment

Local SEO Optimization:

- **Google My Business:** Optimize your Google My Business listing with accurate business information, including location, contact details, and business hours.

- **Local Citations:** Ensure consistency in business information across online directories and local citations.

Monitor and Adjust:

- **Regular Review:** Periodically review the performance of your chosen keywords using analytics tools.

- **Adapt Strategy:** Adjust your strategy based on search trends, customer behavior, and business focus changes.

Track Conversions and ROI[1]:

- **Conversion Tracking:** Implement tracking for website conversions, such as form submissions and phone calls.

- **ROI Analysis:** Assess the return on investment for different keywords and adjust your strategy accordingly.

Stay Informed and Adaptive:

- **Industry Updates:** Stay informed about industry trends, HVAC technology advancements, and changes in customer preferences.

- **Algorithm Changes:** Stay updated on search engine algorithm changes and adapt your strategy accordingly.

Following these steps, you can build a comprehensive HVAC keyword strategy that aligns with your business goals, attracts the right audience, and enhances your online visibility in the competitive HVAC industry. Regularly revisit and refine your strategy to stay ahead in this dynamic digital landscape.

CHAPTER 5:
ON-PAGE OPTIMIZATION TECHNIQUES

On-page optimization is a crucial aspect of SEO that involves optimizing individual web pages to improve their visibility in search engine results and enhance the user experience. Here are critical on-page optimization techniques to implement:

Keyword Research and Placement:

- **Research:** Conduct thorough keyword research to identify relevant and high-search-volume keywords for each page.

- **Placement:** Include target keywords in strategic locations, such as the page title, headings, meta descriptions, and within the content.

Title Tags:

- Optimization: Create compelling and concise title tags for each page.Include Keywords: Place the primary keyword near the beginning of the title tag.

- Length: Keep titles within the recommended word count to ensure visibility in search results.

Meta Descriptions:

- **Clarity and Relevance:** Write clear and relevant meta descriptions that entice users to click.

- **Include Keywords:** Incorporate targeted keywords while maintaining readability.

- **Length:** Keep meta descriptions within the recommended word count to avoid truncation.

Header Tags (H1, H2, H3, etc.):

- **Structure Content:** Use header tags to structure content hierarchically.

- **Include Keywords:** Include relevant keywords in header tags to signal content relevance to search engines.

- **Readability:** Ensure headers enhance content readability for both users and search engines.

URL Structure:

- **Readable URLs[2]:** Create user-friendly and readable URLs.

- **Include Keywords:** Incorporate target keywords in the URL when possible.

- **Avoid Stop Words:** Keep URLs concise by avoiding unnecessary words or stop words.

Optimized Content:

- **Quality Content:** Provide high-quality, valuable, and relevant content for users.

- **Keyword Density:** Maintain a natural keyword density within the content.

- **Semantic Keywords:** Include related terms and synonyms to signal content comprehensiveness.

---

2 Uniform Resource Locator also known as an address on the Web.

Image Optimization:

- **Alt Text:** Include descriptive alt text for images, incorporating relevant keywords.

- **File Size:** Compress images to ensure fast loading times.

- **File Names:** Use descriptive file names that include keywords.

Internal Linking:

- **Relevance:** Create internal links to relevant pages within your website.

- **Anchor Text:** Use descriptive anchor text that provides context for the linked page.

- **User Navigation:** Enhance user navigation by guiding them to related content.

External Linking:

- **High-Quality Sources:** Link to authoritative and relevant external sources.

- **Anchor Text:** Use meaningful anchor text that adds value to the content.

- **User Trust:** Provide additional resources for users to build trust and credibility.

Mobile Optimization:

- **Responsive Design:** Ensure your website is responsive and displays well on various devices.

- **Mobile-Friendly Elements:** Optimize elements such as buttons and fonts for mobile users.

- **Page Speed:** Prioritize mobile page speed for a better user experience.

Page Speed Optimization:

- **Compress Images:** Reduce image file sizes to improve loading times.

- **Minimize HTTP[3] Requests:** Limit the number of server requests by minimizing external resources.

- **Caching:** Implement browser caching to enhance subsequent page loads.

Schema Markup:

- **Rich Snippets:** Use schema markup to provide search engines with additional information about your content.

- **Enhanced SERP Appearance:** Enable rich snippets to improve your appearance in search engine results.

Social Media Integration:

- **Share Buttons:** Include social media share buttons to encourage content sharing.

- **Open Graph Tags:** Implement Open Graph tags for optimized content sharing on platforms like Facebook.

User Experience (UX):

- **Clear Call-to-Action (CTA):** Provide clear CTAs to guide users in taking the desired actions.

- **Readability:** Use legible fonts and maintain a clear hierarchy for easy readability.

- **Avoid Intrusive Pop-ups:** Minimize intrusive pop-ups to improve user experience.

Regular Content Updates:

- **Fresh Content:** Regularly update and add new content to demonstrate website relevance.

---

3 Hypertext Transfer Protocol

- **Recency Signals:** Search engines often favor recently updated content.

HTTPS Protocol:

- **Security:** Ensure your website uses the HTTPS[4] protocol for secure data transmission.

- **Trust Signal:** Google considers HTTPS a ranking signal, enhancing user trust.

Analytics Integration:

- **Google Analytics:** Integrate Google Analytics to track user behavior and monitor website performance.

- **Data-Driven Decisions:** Use analytics data to make informed decisions for ongoing optimization.

By implementing these on-page optimization techniques, you can enhance your website's visibility, user experience, and overall performance in search engine results. Regularly monitor and adapt your strategy to align with evolving SEO best practices and industry trends.

MASTERING TITLE TAGS, META DESCRIPTIONS, AND HEADER TAGS

Mastering title tags, meta descriptions, and header tags is crucial for effective on-page SEO. These elements play a significant role in informing search engines about the content of your page and influencing user click-through rates. Here's a guide to mastering each of these elements:

1. **Title Tags:**

   a. **What They Are:**

      i. The title tag is an HTML element that specifies the title of a web page. It is displayed on search engine results pages (SERPs) as the clickable headline for a result.

---

4 Hypertext Transfer Protocol Secure

b. Best Practices:

    i. Include Target Keywords: Place your primary keyword near the beginning of the title tag.

    ii. Be Concise: Keep title tags concise (around 50-60 characters) to ensure they display correctly in search results.

    iii. Be Compelling: Craft a compelling title that encourages users to click.

    iv. Unique Titles: Ensure each page on your site has a unique and descriptive title.

2. Meta Descriptions:

a. What They Are:

    i. A meta description is a short-lived summary or snippet that provides a concise description of the content of a web page. It appears below the title tag on search engine results pages.

b. Best Practices:

    i. **Include Keywords Naturally:** Integrate relevant keywords naturally into the meta description.

    ii. **Enticing Language:** Write in an enticing and informative manner to encourage users to click.

    iii. **Optimal Length:** To prevent truncation, keep meta descriptions within the recommended length (around 150-160 characters).

    iv. **Unique Descriptions:** To avoid duplicate content issues, create exclusive meta descriptions for each page.

3. **Header Tags (H1, H2, H3, etc.):**

   a. **What They Are:**

      i.   Header tags are HTML elements that define headings and subheadings within your content. The most important headings are H1, H2, H3, etc.

   b. **Best Practices:**

      i.   **H1 for Main Heading:** Use H1 for your page's main title or heading.

      ii. **Hierarchy with Subheadings:** Use H2 for subheadings, and if needed, use H3 for sub-subheadings.

      iii. **Include Keywords:** Incorporate relevant keywords into your headings where it makes sense.

      iv. **Logical Structure:** Ensure a logical hierarchy in your headings to improve content structure.

Tips for Mastery:

1. **Consistency Across Elements:** Maintain consistency in messaging and keywords across title tags, meta descriptions, and header tags. This creates a cohesive and user-friendly experience.

2. **Engage and Encourage Clicks:** Craft compelling and engaging titles and meta descriptions. Use language that encourages users to click on your result.

3. **Balance Optimization and User Experience:** While it's essential to optimize for search engines, prioritize creating a positive user experience. Ensure that your titles and descriptions provide accurate representations of your content.

4. **Regularly Update and Test:** Periodically review and update your title tags and meta descriptions to reflect changes in your

content or business. A/B tests different variations to understand what resonates best with your audience.

5. **Utilize Header Tags for Readability:** Use header tags to break down your content into sections, making it more readable for users and search engines. This enhances the overall user experience.

6. **Leverage Schema Markup:** Implement schema markup where applicable to provide additional context to search engines. This can enhance the visibility of rich snippets in search results.

7. **Monitor Analytics Data:** Use tools like Google Analytics to monitor the performance of your pages. Analyze click-through rates and user behavior to refine your approach.

Remember that mastering these elements is an ongoing process. Stay informed about SEO best practices and algorithm updates to adapt your strategies accordingly. Regularly audit and optimize your on-page factors to maintain relevance and effectiveness in the evolving landscape of search engine optimization.

CRAFTING SEO-OPTIMIZED CONTENT FOR HVAC WEBSITES

Crafting SEO-optimized content for HVAC websites involves creating high-quality, informative, and relevant content that appeals to users and search engines. Here's a step-by-step guide to help you create content that enhances your HVAC website's visibility:

1. **Understand Your Audience and Business:**

    a. **Define Target Audience:** Understand your target audience's demographics, preferences, and needs.

    b. **Know Your Services:** Clearly define the HVAC services your business offers.

2. **Keyword Research:**

   a. **Identify Relevant Keywords:** Conduct keyword research to find terms relevant to HVAC services. Consider location-based keywords for local SEO.

   b. **Long-Tail Keywords:** Include specific, long-tail keywords that address user queries.

3. **Create a Content Plan:**

   a. **Content Categories:** Organize your content into services, maintenance tips, industry trends, and FAQs.

   b. **Keyword Mapping:** Assign target keywords to each piece of content.

4. **Optimize Title Tags and Meta Descriptions:**

   a. **Include Keywords:** Craft compelling title tags that include target keywords.

   b. **Enticing Meta Descriptions:** Write meta descriptions that are both informative and enticing, encouraging users to click.

5. **High-Quality Service Pages:**

   a. **Service Descriptions:** Create detailed pages for each HVAC service you offer. Clearly describe the service, benefits, and why customers should choose your business.

   b. **Localized Content:** Include location-specific information if your services are location-dependent.

6. **Informative Blog Posts:**

   a. **Address Customer Queries:** Write blog posts that address common customer questions and concerns.

   b. **Educational Content:** Provide educational content on HVAC maintenance, energy efficiency, and industry updates.

   c. **Keyword Integration:** Naturally integrate target keywords within the content.

7. Visual Content:

   a. **Images and Infographics:** Use high-quality images and infographics to enhance your content visually.

   b. **Video Content:** Create content showcasing HVAC services, customer testimonials, and maintenance tips.

8. Localized Landing Pages:

   a. **Service Areas:** If your HVAC business serves multiple locations, create dedicated landing pages for each service area.

   b. **Local Testimonials:** Feature testimonials from customers in each service area.

9. Customer Testimonials and Case Studies:

   a. **Build Trust:** Showcase positive customer experiences through testimonials.

   b. **Case Studies:** Highlight successful HVAC projects and their outcomes.

10. Regular Content Updates:

   a. **Stay Current:** Regularly update your content to reflect service changes, industry standards, and technology.

   b. **Seasonal Content:** Provide seasonal tips and promotions to remain relevant throughout the year.

11. FAQs Section:

   a. **Common Queries:** Create a comprehensive FAQ section addressing common queries from customers.

   b. **Keyword Integration:** Include target keywords within FAQ answers.

12. Mobile Optimization:

a. **Responsive Design:** Ensure your website is mobile-friendly for users on various devices.

b. **Mobile-Optimized Content:** Format the content for easy reading on smaller screens.

13. Internal and External Linking:

a. **Internal Links:** Create internal links to connect related content within your website.

b. **External Links:** Provide a link to authoritative sources to add credibility to your content.

14. Social Media Integration:

a. **Shareable Content:** Create content that is shareable on social media platforms.

b. **Social Proof:** Share customer testimonials and project photos on social media.

15. Schema Markup:

a. **Rich Snippets:** Implement schema markup to enhance the visibility of rich snippets in search results.

16. Call-to-Action (CTA):

a. **Clear CTAs:** Include clear calls-to-action on service pages, encouraging users to contact or request services.

17. Regularly Monitor Analytics:

a. **Google Analytics:** Track user engagement, page views, and conversion rates.

b. **Adjust Strategy:** Use analytics data to refine your content strategy over time.

18. **Adapt to Algorithm Changes:**

   a. **Stay Informed:** Stay updated on search engine algorithm changes and adjust your strategy accordingly.

Crafting SEO-optimized content is an ongoing process. Regularly analyze performance metrics, update content based on user feedback and industry changes, and adapt your strategy to ensure sustained visibility in search engine results.

IMAGE OPTIMIZATION FOR IMPROVED SEO PERFORMANCE

Image optimization is crucial for improving SEO performance as it enhances the user experience and contributes to faster page load times and better search engine rankings. Here are key practices for image optimization:

1. **Choose the Right File Format:**

   a. **JPEG for Photographs:** Use JPEG for high-quality photographs as it provides a good balance between image quality and file size.

   b. **PNG for Graphics and Logos:** Use PNG for transparent images or graphics and logos.

   c. **WebP for Modern Browsers:** Consider using WebP, a modern image format with good compression without compromising quality. However, it may not be supported by all browsers.

2. **Optimize Image Dimensions:**

   a. **Resize Images:** Ensure images are resized to the dimensions needed on the webpage. Avoid using large images and then scaling them down in HTML or CSS.

b. **Responsive Images:** Implement responsive design techniques to serve appropriately sized images based on the user's device.

3. Compress Images:

a. **Lossless Compression:** Use tools like ImageOptim or TinyPNG for lossless compression to reduce file sizes without sacrificing image quality.

b. **Balancing Quality and Size:** Adjust compression settings to find the right balance between image quality and file size.

4. Use Descriptive Filenames:

a. **Keyword-Rich Filenames:** Rename image files with descriptive, keyword-rich filenames. Avoid generic names like "image001.jpg."

b. **Hyphens Instead of Underscores:** Use hyphens (-) instead of underscores (_) to separate words in filenames.

5. Utilize Alt Text:

a. **Descriptive Alt Text:** Add descriptive alt text to each image. Alt text should concisely describe the content and purpose of the image.

b. **Incorporate Keywords Naturally:** If relevant, include target keywords in the alt text, but do so naturally.

6. Enable Image Compression in CMS:

a. **Automated Compression:** If using a content management system (CMS), explore plugins or settings that automatically compress images upon upload.

7. Implement Lazy Loading:

a. **Lazy Loading Plugins:** Implement lazy loading to defer the loading of images until they are about to come into the user's viewport. Many CMS platforms and plugins offer built-in lazy loading options.

8. Image Sitemaps:

a. **Include Images in Sitemaps:** If applicable, include images in your XML sitemap to help search engines discover and index them.

9. Choose the Right Color Profile:

a. **RGB for Web:** Use the RGB color profile for images intended for the web. Avoid using CMYK, which is designed for print.

10. Consider Image CDN:

a. **Content Delivery Network (CDN):** Use a CDN to serve images from servers geographically closer to the user, reducing latency and improving load times.

11. Caption and Context:

a. **Provide Context:** If using captions, ensure they provide context to the image. Captions can be an additional opportunity to include relevant keywords.

12. Review Performance Regularly:

a. **Page Speed Insights:** Regularly check your website's performance using tools like Google PageSpeed Insights. Address any issues related to image loading times.

13. Social Media Sharing Tags:

a. **Open Graph Tags:** If your images are shared on social media, use Open Graph tags to control how the content appears when shared on platforms like Facebook.

14. Image Watermarking:

a. **Considerations for Watermarks:** Ensure they do not distract from the main content or negatively impact the user experience.

15. Test on Different Devices:

a. **Cross-Browser Compatibility:** Test how images load on different browsers and devices to ensure a consistent user experience.

Optimizing images is not only beneficial for SEO but also for user engagement. These best practices can enhance your website's performance, reduce bounce rates, and improve your overall search engine rankings. Regularly review and update your image optimization strategy to align with evolving best practices and technologies.

CHAPTER 6:

OFF-PAGE OPTIMIZATION STRATEGIES

Off-page optimization refers to activities performed outside of your website but contributes to its overall visibility and authority on the internet. Here are key off-page optimization strategies to improve your website's SEO and online reputation:

1. Link Building:

a. **High-Quality Backlinks:** Acquire high-quality, relevant backlinks from authoritative websites in your industry.

b. **Diverse Anchor Text:** Use various anchor texts that include your target keywords, branded terms, and natural phrases.

c. **Guest Blogging:** Contribute guest posts to reputable websites within your niche, including a link to your site.

2. Social Media Marketing:

a. **Social Signals:** Maintain an active presence on major social media platforms. Social signals like likes, shares, and comments can indirectly influence search rankings.

b. **Link Sharing:** Share your content on social media to encourage engagement and increase the likelihood of others linking to it.

3. Influencer Marketing:

a. **Collaborate with Influencers:** Partner with influencers in your industry who can promote your content or products to their followers.

b. **Co-Create Content:** Work with influencers to co-create content, such as blog posts, videos, or social media campaigns.

4. Brand Mentions and Citations:

a. **Online Directories:** Ensure your business information is consistent across online directories and local citation sites.

b. **Monitor Brand Mentions:** Track mentions of your brand online and reach out to sites that mention you without providing a link, requesting them to add one.

5. Content Marketing:

a. **Create Linkable Content:** Develop high-quality, informative, and shareable content that naturally attracts links.

b. **Infographics and Visual Content:** Create visually appealing content, such as easily shareable infographics, for use on other websites.

6. Online Reviews and Testimonials:

a. **Encourage Reviews:** Encourage satisfied customers to leave positive reviews on review sites, Google My Business, and social media.

b. **Respond to Reviews:** Address negative reviews professionally and respond to positive ones to engage with your audience.

7. Forum Participation and Blog Commenting:

a. **Industry Forums:** Participate in industry forums and communities. Share your expertise and include a link to your website in your forum signature.

b. **Blog Comments:** Thoughtfully engage in blog comments on relevant websites. Avoid spammy comments and focus on adding value to discussions.

8. Local SEO Strategies:

a. **Local Citations:** Ensure your business is listed accurately on local directories and citation sites.

b. **Local Link Building:** Build relationships with local businesses and organizations and seek opportunities for local link building.

9. Community Engagement:

a. **Sponsorships:** Sponsor local events or community organizations, which can lead to brand exposure and potential backlinks.

b. **Participate in Events:** In industry events, conferences, and meetups to build connections.

10. Press Releases:

a. **Newsworthy Updates:** Issue press releases for significant events, achievements, or product launches. Distribute them through reputable press release distribution services.

11. Broken Link Building:

a. **Identify Broken Links:** Find broken links on other websites in your niche.

b. **Reach Out for Replacement:** Contact the site owner, notify them of the broken link, and suggest your content as a replacement.

12. Social Bookmarking:

a. **Share Content:** Share your content on social bookmarking sites like Reddit, StumbleUpon, or Digg.

b. **Participate in Communities:** Join relevant communities on these platforms and contribute to discussions.

13. Video Marketing:

a. **YouTube Optimization:** Optimize your YouTube channel and videos for search. Include relevant keywords in titles, descriptions, and tags.

b. **Embed Videos:** Embed videos on your website and encourage others to do the same.

14. Q&A Platforms:

a. **Participate in Q&A Sites:** Provide helpful answers on Quora or industry-specific Q&A sites. Include a link to your relevant content when appropriate.

15. Ego Bait:

a. **Mentions of Influencers:** Create content that mentions or features influencers in your industry. Notify them about it, increasing the likelihood of them sharing it.

16. Document Sharing:

a. **SlideShare and PDFs:** Create informative presentations or PDF documents and share them on platforms like SlideShare or document-sharing sites.

17. Monitoring and Analysis:

a. **Backlink Monitoring:** Regularly monitor your backlink profile using tools like Ahrefs or Moz.

b. **Analyze Performance:** Using analytics tools, assess the impact of off-page strategies on your website's performance.

18. Stay Current with SEO Trends:

a. **Algorithm Updates:** Stay informed about search engine algorithm updates and adjust your strategies accordingly.

Effective off-page optimization requires a strategic and ethical approach. Focus on building a natural link profile, fostering a positive online reputation, and engaging with your target audience across various platforms. Regularly assess the effectiveness of your off-page strategies and adapt them to align with evolving SEO trends and industry changes.

BUILDING HIGH-QUALITY BACKLINKS FOR HVAC WEBSITES

Building high-quality backlinks is essential for improving the SEO performance of HVAC websites. Here are effective strategies for acquiring quality backlinks in the HVAC industry:

1. Create High-Quality Content:

a. **Informative Blog Posts:** Produce informative and shareable blog posts about HVAC industry trends, energy efficiency, maintenance tips, and common problems.

b. **Visual Content:** Create visually appealing infographics, videos, and slideshows that other websites want to link to.

2. Collaborate with Industry Influencers:

a. **Expert Interviews:** Interview HVAC industry influencers or experts and feature them on your website.

b. **Collaborative Content:** Collaborate with influencers to co-create content, including joint blog posts, videos, and webinars.

3. Local Business Directories:

a. **Local Citations:** Ensure your HVAC business is listed accurately on local business directories and citation sites.

b. **Niche Directories:** Submit your website to HVAC-specific directories and industry associations.

4. Guest Blogging:

    a. **Identify Opportunities:** Find reputable websites related to HVAC that accept guest posts.

    b. **Quality Content:** Write high-quality, informative guest posts with links to your website in the author bio or within the content.

5. Participate in Industry Forums:

    a. **Engage in Discussions:** Actively participate in HVAC industry forums and discussion boards.

    b. **Signature Links:** Include a link to your website in the forum signature, but do so in a non-spammy manner.

6. Local Sponsorships and Events:

    a. **Sponsor Local Events:** Sponsor local HVAC-related events, community gatherings, or sports teams.

    b. **Event Participation:** Participate actively in local industry events and trade shows.

7. Resource and Tools Pages:

    a. **Linkable Resources:** Create valuable resources such as guides, checklists, or tools that other websites in the HVAC industry might find helpful.

    b. **Outreach:** Reach out to relevant websites and inform them about your resource, encouraging them to link to it.

8. Repair Broken Links:

    a. **Identify Broken Links:** Use tools like Ahrefs or Check My Links to find broken links on HVAC-related websites.

    b. **Provide Replacement Content:** Reach out to site owners, notify them of the broken link, and suggest your content as a replacement.

9. Online Reviews and Testimonials:

a. Testimonial Link Building: Provide positive testimonials to HVAC suppliers, manufacturers, or service providers in exchange for a link to your website.

b. Local Business Review Sites: Encourage satisfied customers to leave reviews on local business review sites that allow you to include a link.

10. Community Engagement:

a. Participate in Local Communities: Get involved in local community forums, social media groups, and online communities where discussions about HVAC services may occur.

b. Networking: Build relationships with other local businesses, and they may naturally link to your website.

11. Create Shareable Content:

a. Shareable Infographics: Design shareable infographics related to HVAC tips, energy efficiency, or industry statistics.

b. How-to Guides: Develop comprehensive guides that other websites might reference and link to.

12. Educational Outreach:

a. Offer Workshops: Offer educational workshops or webinars about HVAC maintenance, energy efficiency, or related topics.

b. School Partnerships: Partner with local schools or community colleges to provide educational content, and they may link to your resources.

13. Social Media Engagement:

a. Shareable Content: Share your HVAC content on social media platforms to increase visibility and encourage sharing.

b. **Engage with Influencers:** Engage with HVAC industry influencers on social media, and they may notice and link to your content.

14. Online Press Releases:

a. **Industry Updates:** Issue online press releases for significant updates, achievements, or contributions to the HVAC industry.

b. **Distribute through PR Platforms:** Distribute press releases through reputable online distribution platforms.

15. Linkable Case Studies:

a. **Highlight Success Stories:** Create case studies showcasing successful HVAC projects or unique solutions.

b. **Outreach to Relevant Sites:** Reach out to relevant websites, especially those in construction or home improvement niches, and share your case studies.

16. Ego Bait:

a. **Mentions of Industry Leaders:** Create content that mentions or features well-known HVAC industry leaders or companies.

b. **Notify and Outreach:** Notify the mentioned entities, and they might link to the content or share it.

17. Utilize HVAC Associations:

a. **Association Memberships:** Join HVAC associations and organizations. Many of them have member directories where you can get a link to your website.

b. **Participate in Events:** Attend association events and conferences, and they may link to your website as a participant.

18. Monitor Competitors:

a. **Competitor Backlink Analysis:** Analyze your competitors' backlink profiles to identify potential link-building opportunities.

b. **Improve Existing Content:** If competitors have similar content with more backlinks, consider improving your content and reaching out for links.

Remember to prioritize quality over quantity when building backlinks. Focus on acquiring links from reputable and relevant sources within the HVAC industry. Regularly monitor your backlink profile and adapt your strategies to align with industry trends and search engine guidelines.

THE ROLE OF SOCIAL MEDIA INTEGRATION IN HVAC SEO

Social media integration significantly impacts HVAC SEO by increasing online visibility, brand awareness, and engagement. While social signals themselves may not have a direct impact on search engine rankings, a well-executed social media strategy can indirectly influence SEO in several ways:

1. Increased Brand Visibility:

a. **Social Sharing:** When shared on social media platforms, HVAC content reaches a broader audience and exposes the brand to potential customers.

b. **Brand Recognition:** Increased visibility on social media contributes to brand recognition, which can lead to more branded searches and improved search engine performance.

2. Content Distribution and Amplification:

a. **Broader Reach:** Social media provides a platform for distributing HVAC-related content to a larger audience.

b. **Content Amplification:** When users share, like, or comment on your content, it amplifies its reach and potential impact on SEO.

3. Building Backlinks:

a. **Shared Content:** When shared on social media, HVAC content can attract backlinks from other websites that find the content valuable.

b. **Social Signals:** While the direct impact of social signals on SEO is debated, quality content that gains traction on social media may attract attention and backlinks.

4. Local SEO Benefits:

a. **Google Business Profile:** An active and optimized social media presence can complement your Google Business profile, contributing to local SEO.

b. **Local Engagement:** Engaging with the local community on social media can enhance your visibility in local search results.

5. Customer Reviews and Testimonials:

a. **Local SEO Impact:** Positive reviews and testimonials on social media platforms contribute to a positive online reputation, impacting local SEO.

b. **User-Generated Content:** Encouraging customers to share their experiences on social media generates user-generated content that can positively influence SEO.

6. Social Signals and Brand Authority:

a. **Brand Authority:** While not a direct ranking factor, a strong social media presence can enhance brand authority, making your HVAC business appear more credible to search engines.

b. **Credibility Signals:** Social signals, such as followers, likes, and shares, can contribute to perceived credibility and authority.

7. Content Indexing:

a. **Social Media Content Indexing:** Some search engines also index social media content. A well-optimized social media profile with relevant information can improve visibility.

8. Local Community Engagement:

a. **Local Events:** Promoting and engaging in local events on social media can foster connections within the community, positively impacting local SEO.

b. **Community Trust:** Active participation in local discussions and events builds trust, influencing customer decisions and potentially leading to more local searches.

9. Social Proof and Trust Building:

a. **Customer Testimonials:** Positive testimonials and reviews on social media platforms serve as social proof, building trust with potential customers.

b. **Transparency:** Social media allows HVAC businesses to showcase transparency, responsiveness, and customer-centric values, contributing to trust.

10. Social Media Signals for Crawlers:

a. **Search Engine Crawlers:** Social media signals, such as the frequency of content updates and engagement metrics, can be considered by search engine crawlers in evaluating the freshness and relevance of content.

11. Optimizing Social Profiles for SEO:

a. **Keyword Optimization:** Ensure your social media profiles are optimized with relevant keywords related to HVAC services and your location.

b. **Consistent NAP Information:** Consistency in business information (Name, Address, Phone) across social media and other online platforms supports local SEO efforts.

12. User Engagement Metrics:

a. **User Engagement:** Social media metrics, such as likes, shares, and comments, can indirectly influence user engagement metrics that search engines consider.

b. **Brand Mentions:** Mentions of your brand on social media contribute to a positive online presence.

13. Social Media Advertising:

a. **Targeted Advertising:** Social media advertising allows HVAC businesses to target specific demographics, increasing the chances of reaching the right audience.

b. **Brand Exposure:** Paid social media campaigns can increase brand exposure and indirectly impact search behavior.

14. Monitoring Social Analytics:

a. **Analyzing Performance:** Regularly monitor social media analytics to understand what content resonates with your audience. Use insights to refine your content strategy.

15. Integrating Social Media with Content Strategy:

a. **Content Sharing:** Integrate social media sharing buttons on your HVAC website to encourage users to share your content.

b. **Cross-Promotion:** Promote HVAC blog posts, articles, or guides on social media platforms to drive traffic to your website.

16. User Engagement on Social Platforms:

a. **Interactive Content:** Create interactive content on social media, such as polls or quizzes, to encourage engagement and discussion.

b. **Respond to Queries:** Promptly respond to user queries and comments on social media to build positive interactions.

In summary, social media integration complements HVAC SEO efforts by enhancing brand visibility, supporting local SEO, building backlinks, and fostering positive customer relationships. A holistic digital marketing strategy that includes both SEO and social media can lead to a more robust online presence and increased opportunities for customer acquisition. Regularly assess the performance of your social media efforts and adjust strategies to align with your SEO goals.

INFLUENCER COLLABORATIONS AND THEIR IMPACT ON SEO

Social media integration significantly impacts HVAC SEO by increasing online visibility, brand awareness, and engagement. While social signals themselves may not have a direct impact on search engine rankings, a well-executed social media strategy can indirectly influence SEO in several ways:

1. Increased Brand Visibility:

a. **Social Sharing:** When shared on social media platforms, HVAC content reaches a broader audience and exposes the brand to potential customers.

b. **Brand Recognition:** Increased visibility on social media contributes to brand recognition, which can lead to more branded searches and improved search engine performance.

2. Content Distribution and Amplification:

a. **Wider Reach:** Social media provides a platform for distributing HVAC-related content to a larger audience.

b. **Content Amplification:** When users share, like, or comment on your content, it amplifies its reach and potential impact on SEO.

3. Building Backlinks:

a. **Shared Content:** When shared on social media, HVAC content can attract backlinks from other websites that find the content valuable.

b. **Social Signals:** While the direct impact of social signals on SEO is debated, quality content that gains traction on social media may attract attention and backlinks.

4. Local SEO Benefits:

a. **Google Business Profile (GBP):** An active and optimized social media presence can complement your Google My Business profile, contributing to local SEO.

b. **Local Engagement:** Engaging with the local community on social media can enhance your visibility in local search results.

5. Customer Reviews and Testimonials:

a. **Local SEO Impact:** Positive reviews and testimonials on social media platforms contribute to a positive online reputation, impacting local SEO.

b. **User-Generated Content:** Encouraging customers to share their experiences on social media generates user-generated content that can positively influence SEO.

6. Social Signals and Brand Authority:

a. **Brand Authority:** While not a direct ranking factor, a strong social media presence can enhance brand authority, making your HVAC business appear more credible to search engines.

b. **Credibility Signals:** Social signals, such as followers, likes, and shares, can contribute to perceived credibility and authority.

7. Content Indexing:

a. Social Media Content Indexing: Some search engines also index social media content. A well-optimized social media profile with relevant information can improve visibility.

8. Local Community Engagement:

a. Local Events: Promoting and engaging in local events on social media can foster connections within the community, positively impacting local SEO.

b. Community Trust: Active participation in local discussions and events builds trust, influencing customer decisions and potentially leading to more local searches.

9. Social Proof and Trust Building:

a. Customer Testimonials: Positive testimonials and reviews on social media platforms serve as social proof, building trust with potential customers.

b. Transparency: Social media allows HVAC businesses to showcase transparency, responsiveness, and customer-centric values, contributing to trust.

10. Social Media Signals for Crawlers:

a. Search Engine Crawlers: Social media signals, such as the frequency of content updates and engagement metrics, can be considered by search engine crawlers in evaluating the freshness and relevance of content.

11. Optimizing Social Profiles for SEO:

a. Keyword Optimization: Ensure your social media profiles are optimized with relevant keywords related to HVAC services and your location.

b. Consistent NAP Information: Consistency in business information (Name, Address, Phone) across social media and other online platforms supports local SEO efforts.

12. User Engagement Metrics:

a. **User Engagement:** Social media metrics, such as likes, shares, and comments, can indirectly influence user engagement metrics that search engines consider.

b. **Brand Mentions:** Mentions of your brand on social media contribute to a positive online presence.

13. Social Media Advertising:

a. **Targeted Advertising:** Social media advertising allows HVAC businesses to target specific demographics, increasing the chances of reaching the right audience.

b. **Brand Exposure:** Paid social media campaigns can increase brand exposure and indirectly impact search behavior.

14. Monitoring Social Analytics:

a. **Analyzing Performance:** Regularly monitor social media analytics to understand what content resonates with your audience. Use insights to refine your content strategy.

15. Integrating Social Media with Content Strategy:

a. **Content Sharing:** Integrate social media sharing buttons on your HVAC website to encourage users to share your content.

b. **Cross-Promotion:** Promote HVAC blog posts, articles, or guides on social media platforms to drive traffic to your website.

16. User Engagement on Social Platforms:

a. **Interactive Content:** Create interactive content on social media, such as polls or quizzes, to encourage engagement and discussion.

b. **Respond to Queries:** Promptly respond to user queries and comments on social media to build positive interactions.

In summary, social media integration complements HVAC SEO efforts by enhancing brand visibility, supporting local SEO, building backlinks, and fostering positive customer relationships. A holistic digital marketing strategy that includes both SEO and social media can lead to a more robust online presence and increased opportunities for customer acquisition. Regularly assess the performance of your social media efforts and adjust strategies to align with your SEO goals.

CHAPTER 7:

LOCAL SEO TACTICS FOR HVAC DEALERS

Local SEO is crucial for HVAC dealers to ensure that their business is visible to potential customers in their local area. Here are effective local SEO tactics tailored for HVAC dealers:

1. Optimize your profile on Google Business Profile (GBP):

    a. **Complete Business Information:** Ensure your GBP profile is fully optimized with an accurate business name, address, phone number (NAP), and other relevant details.

    b. **Service Areas:** Specify the geographic areas you serve to improve local search relevance.

2. Local Keyword Optimization:

    a. **Keyword Research:** Identify and target local keywords relevant to HVAC services in your area.

    b. **Include Location in Content:** Integrate local keywords naturally into your website content, meta tags, and headings.

3. Localized Content on the Website:

    a. **Service Pages for Locations:** Create dedicated pages for each service area on your website, providing specific information about the HVAC services offered in each location.

b. **Local Testimonials:** Showcase customer testimonials and case studies specific to each service area.

4. Local Citations and Directories:

a. **Consistent NAP Information:** Ensure that your business name, address, and phone number are consistent across all online directories and citation sites.

b. **HVAC Directories:** List your business on HVAC-specific directories and local business directories.

5. Online Reviews and Ratings:

a. **Positive Reviews:** Encourage satisfied customers to leave positive reviews on your GBP profile and other review platforms.

b. **Respond to Reviews:** Respond promptly and professionally to positive and negative reviews.

6. Local Link Building:

a. **Local Partnerships:** Build relationships with local businesses and organizations for potential link-building opportunities.

b. **Local Events:** Sponsor or participate in local events and community activities, gaining exposure and potential backlinks.

7. Schema Markup for HVAC:

a. **Implement Schema Markup:** Use schema markup to provide search engines with detailed information about your HVAC services, service areas, and contact details.

b. **Rich Snippets:** Enhance your search results with rich snippets that display additional information, such as reviews and service hours.

8. Mobile Optimization:

a. **Responsive Design:** Ensure your website is mobile-friendly, as many users search for HVAC services on mobile devices.

b. **Mobile Page Speed:** Optimize page load times for mobile users to improve user experience.

9. Local Content Marketing:

a. **Local Blog Posts:** Create blog posts addressing local HVAC concerns, seasonal tips, and industry news relevant to your service areas.

b. **Local Case Studies:** Showcase successful HVAC projects in specific locations with details about challenges and solutions.

10. Google Posts:

a. **Regular Updates:** Use Google Posts within your GBP profile to share updates, promotions, and announcements.

b. **Engage with Customers:** Encourage customer interaction on Google Posts with calls-to-action.

11. Local SEO for Voice Search:

a. **Conversational Keywords:** Optimize content for voice search by incorporating conversational and long-tail keywords.

b. **FAQs for Voice Search:** Create an FAQ section on your website with questions and answers structured for voice search.

12. Social Media Presence:

a. **Localized Social Content:** Share localized content on social media platforms that highlights your services and community involvement.**Engage with Local Audience:** Respond to comments and messages, and engage with your local audience on social media.

13. Local SEO Analytics:

a. **Track Local Rankings:** Monitor your search rankings for targeted keywords using tools like Google Analytics and Google Search Console.

b. **Analyze Local Traffic:** Understand the sources of local traffic and user behavior on your website.

14. Local SEO for Google Maps:

a. **Optimized Map Listing:** Ensure your business location is accurately marked on Google Maps.

b. **Encourage Map Reviews:** Ask satisfied customers to leave reviews directly on your Google Maps listing.

15. Localized PPC Campaigns:

a. **Geo-Targeted Ads:** Run pay-per-click (PPC) campaigns with geo-targeting settings to reach users specifically in your service areas.

b. **Localized Landing Pages:** Create specific landing pages for each location targeted in your PPC campaigns.

16. Regular Website Audits:

a. **Technical SEO Check:** Perform regular audits to address technical SEO issues, including broken links, page load times, and crawl errors.

b. **Local SEO Updates:** Keep your website's local SEO strategies up-to-date with changing algorithms and trends.

17. Local Voice Search Optimization:

a. **Natural Language Content:** Optimize content to match the natural language used in voice searches.

b. **Featured Snippets:** Aim for featured snippets in search results to increase visibility in voice search.

Local SEO for HVAC dealers requires a comprehensive approach integrating on-page and off-page strategies. Consistency, accuracy, and relevance across all online platforms are vital in establishing a strong local online presence and attracting local customers. Regularly assess and refine your local SEO tactics to stay competitive in the local market.

OPTIMIZING GOOGLE MY BUSINESS FOR LOCAL HVAC VISIBILITY

Optimizing your profile on Google Business Profile (GBP) profile is crucial for improving local visibility for your HVAC business. A well-optimized GBP profile can increase your chances of appearing in local search results and attracting potential customers. Here are steps to optimize your Google Business Profile listing for local HVAC visibility:

1. Claim and Verify Your Listing:

a. **Claim Your Business:** If you haven't already, claim ownership of your HVAC business on Google My Business.

b. **Verification:** Complete the verification process to confirm that you are the rightful owner.

2. Complete Your Business Information:

a. **Accurate NAP:** Ensure your business name, address, and phone number (NAP) are correct and consistent and match the information on your website and other online platforms.

b. **Business Hours:** Provide accurate and up-to-date business hours, including any special hours for holidays or events.

3. Choose the Right Business Categories:

a. **Primary and Secondary Categories:** Select your HVAC business's most relevant primary category. Add additional categories if applicable.

b. **Be Specific:** Choose specific categories that accurately describe your services.

4. Write a Compelling Business Description:

a. **Informative Content:** Write a concise business description highlighting your HVAC services, experience, and unique selling points.

b. **Keywords:** Incorporate relevant keywords naturally, but avoid keyword stuffing.

5. Add High-Quality Photos:

a. **Profile Photo:** Use a high-quality and professional-looking logo or profile picture.

b. **Cover Photo:** Add a visually appealing cover photo representing your HVAC business.

c. **Service Photos:** Include photos of your team, service vehicles, completed projects, and the interior and exterior of your business.

6. Collect and Respond to Reviews:

a. **Encourage Reviews:** Encourage satisfied customers to leave positive reviews on your GBP profile.

b. **Respond to Reviews:** Respond promptly and professionally to all positive and negative reviews to show engagement and customer care.

7. Utilize Google Posts:

a. **Regular Updates:** Use Google Posts to share updates, promotions, and relevant content about your HVAC business.

b. **Calls-to-Action:** Include calls-to-action in your posts, such as "Learn More" or "Call Now."

8. Include Relevant Attributes:

a. **Attributes Section:** Use the attributes section to highlight specific features or services offered by your HVAC business (e.g., women-led, veteran-led, offers financing).

b. **COVID-19 Information:** If applicable, provide information about any safety measures or changes due to COVID-19.

9. Enable Messaging:

a. **Messaging Feature:** Enable the messaging feature to allow potential customers to contact you through your GBP profile.

b. **Respond Promptly:** Respond to messages promptly to provide excellent customer service.

10. Create and Monitor Q&A:

a. **Add Frequently Asked Questions:** Anticipate common questions about your HVAC services and add them to the Q&A section.

b. **Monitor and Respond:** Regularly check and respond to user-generated questions on your GBP listing.

11. Manage and Update Information:

a. **Regular Updates:** Keep your GBP information up-to-date, especially if there are changes to your business hours, location, or services.

b. **Seasonal Updates:** Update your GBP profile with seasonal promotions or offers.

12. Utilize Services Menu (if applicable):

a. **List Your Services:** If your HVAC business offers specific services, use the services menu feature to provide detailed information and pricing.

b. **Service Descriptions:** Include clear and concise descriptions for each service.

13. Monitor Insights and Analytics:

a. **GBP Insights:** Regularly check the insights and analytics Google My Business provides to understand how users interact with your listing.

    b. **Refine Strategies:** Use the data to refine your local SEO and business strategies.

14. Integrate Appointment Booking:

    a. **Appointment Link:** If applicable, integrate an appointment booking link that directs users to your online scheduling system.

    b. **Online Booking Platforms:** Connect your GBP profile to popular online booking platforms if you use them.

15. Optimize for Local SEO Keywords:

    a. **Local Keywords:** Integrate local HVAC-related keywords naturally into your business description, posts, and services.

    b. **Localized Content:** Create localized content on your website and link to it from your GBP profile.

16. Link to Relevant Pages on Your Website:

    a. **Website URL:** Include a link to your website's homepage or a specific landing page that provides valuable information about your HVAC services.

    b. **Use UTM Parameters:** If tracking is necessary, use UTM parameters for your website link to monitor traffic from your GBP profile.

17. Regularly Audit Your GBP Listing:

    a. **Regular Audits:** Conduct regular audits of your GBP listing to ensure that all information is accurate and up-to-date.

    b. **Fix Inaccuracies:** Address any inaccuracies or issues promptly.

Following these optimization strategies can enhance your HVAC business's visibility on Google My Business and improve your chances of attracting local customers. Consistent monitoring and updates are crucial to maintaining a compelling and informative GBP profile for your HVAC business.

HARNESSING THE POWER OF LOCAL CITATIONS AND REVIEWS

Harnessing the power of local citations and reviews is essential for improving your HVAC business's online visibility and reputation. Both local citations and reviews play significant roles in local search rankings, user trust, and customer acquisition. Here's how you can effectively utilize local citations and reviews for your HVAC business:

Local Citations:

1. What Are Local Citations?

a. **Definition:** Local citations are online mentions of your business name, address, and phone number (NAP) on various websites, directories, and platforms.

b. **Types of Citations:** Citations can be structured (found on business directories) or unstructured (mentions on blogs, news articles, social media, etc.).

2. Optimizing Local Citations:

a. **Consistent NAP Information:** Ensure that your business name, address, and phone number are consistent across all local citations and match the information on your website.

b. **Complete Citations:** Provide as much information as possible when creating citations, including business hours, website URL, and a brief business description.

3. Popular Citation Sources:

a. **Google My Business:** Optimize and maintain your Google My Business profile, as it is a crucial citation source and a significant factor in local search rankings.

b. **Google Reviews, Yelp, Yellow Pages, and Other Directories:** List your HVAC business on popular business directories relevant to your industry.

4. Industry-Specific Directories:

a. **HVAC Directories:** Identify and list your business on HVAC-specific directories or industry associations.

b. **Local Chambers of Commerce:** Join local chambers of commerce and ensure your business information is listed on their websites.

5. Monitor and Update Citations:

a. **Regular Audits:** Conduct regular audits to identify and correct any inconsistencies or inaccuracies in your citations.

b. **Niche Citations:** Identify niche-specific directories related to heating, ventilation, and air conditioning and ensure your business is listed.

6. Local SEO Benefits:

a. **Local Search Rankings:** Consistent and accurate citations improve local search rankings.

b. **Map Pack Inclusion:** Well-optimized citations increase the likelihood of your HVAC business appearing in local map packs on SERPs.

7. Localized Content in Citations:

a. **Local Keywords:** Include local keywords naturally in your citation descriptions to enhance local relevance.

b. **Service Area Information:** Specify the geographic areas you serve within your citations.

Reviews:

1. Importance of Online Reviews:

a. **Customer Trust:** Reviews build trust and credibility with potential customers. Positive reviews can influence decision-making.

b. **Local SEO Impact:** Reviews are a factor in local search ranking algorithms.

2. Encouraging Positive Reviews:

a. **Provide Excellent Service:** Consistently deliver exceptional service to customers to increase the likelihood of positive reviews.

b. **Ask Satisfied Customers:** Politely ask satisfied customers to leave positive reviews on platforms like Google, Trustpilot, Yelp, and other relevant sites.

3. Optimizing Responses to Reviews:

a. **Respond Promptly:** Respond to both positive and negative reviews promptly and professionally.

b. **Address Concerns:** If a customer expresses a concern, address it in your response and show a willingness to resolve it.

4. Diversify Review Sources:

a. **Google Reviews:** Prioritize Google Reviews due to their impact on local SEO.

b. **Other Platforms:** Encourage customers to leave reviews on multiple platforms like Yelp, Facebook, and industry-specific sites.

5. Leverage Happy Customers for Testimonials:

a. **Website Testimonials:** Feature positive reviews and testimonials on your HVAC website.

b. **Showcase Success Stories:** Share specific success stories or projects with customer permission.

6. Utilize Customer Feedback for Improvement:

a. **Feedback Analysis:** Analyze customer feedback from reviews to identify areas for improvement in your HVAC services.

b. **Continuous Improvement:** Use constructive feedback to enhance customer satisfaction and business operations.

7. Incorporate Reviews in Marketing Materials:

a. **Social Proof:** Highlight positive reviews in your HVAC marketing materials, such as brochures, flyers, and digital campaigns.

b. **Customer Stories:** Share customer stories and testimonials in your marketing efforts.

8. Local SEO and Review Signals:

a. **Local Search Impact:** Positive reviews increase your business's visibility in local search results.

b. **Review Quantity and Diversity:** Aim for a diverse and substantial number of reviews across various platforms.

9. Monitor Online Review Platforms:

a. **Set Up Alerts:** Use tools or alerts to be notified of new reviews on various platforms.

b. **Timely Responses:** Respond to reviews promptly, demonstrating your commitment to customer feedback.

10. Educate Customers on Leaving Reviews:

a. **Provide Instructions:** Offer simple instructions or links on your website or follow-up emails on how customers can leave reviews.

b. **Make it Easy:** Streamline the review process to encourage more customers to share their experiences.

11. Address Negative Reviews Professionally:

a. **Stay Professional:** Maintain a professional tone when responding to negative reviews.

b. **Resolve Issues Privately:** When possible, address and resolve customer issues privately to show dedication to customer satisfaction.

12. Use Customer Testimonials in SEO Content:

a. **Content Integration:** Integrate positive reviews and testimonials like service pages and case studies into your website's content.

b. **Structured Data Markup:** Consider using structured data markup to highlight reviews in search engine results.

13. Create a Review Acquisition Strategy:

a. **Email Campaigns:** Implement email campaigns to request reviews from satisfied customers.

b. **In-Person Requests:** Train your staff to request reviews from happy customers during in-person interactions.

14. Highlight Local Projects and Success Stories:

a. **Localized Content:** Create website content highlighting successful HVAC projects in specific service areas.

b. **Link to Reviews:** Link to relevant reviews within the content to provide social proof.

15. Legal and Ethical Considerations:

a. **Follow Guidelines:** Adhere to the guidelines and policies of review platforms when encouraging and responding to reviews.

b. **Avoid Fake Reviews:** Never engage in or encourage the creation of fake reviews, as it can harm your business reputation.

Your HVAC business can enhance its online presence by strategically managing local citations and reviews, building trust with potential customers, and improving local search rankings. Regularly monitor and adapt your strategies to stay competitive in the local market and maintain a positive online reputation.

GEO-TARGETED CONTENT STRATEGIES FOR LOCAL SEO

Geo-targeted content strategies are crucial for HVAC businesses looking to enhance their local SEO efforts. Localized content helps your business connect with the community, improves relevance in local search results, and engages potential customers. Here are effective geo-targeted content strategies for local SEO:

1. Create Location-Specific Service Pages:

a. **Dedicated Pages:** Develop dedicated service pages for each location you serve, providing detailed information about HVAC services available in that area.

b. **Local Keywords:** Integrate local keywords naturally into these pages' content, meta tags, and headers.

2. Localized Blog Content:

a. **Community-Centric Blog Posts:** Create blog posts focusing on community events, news, and topics relevant to your specific locations.

b. **Seasonal Tips:** Provide seasonal HVAC maintenance tips tailored to the climate of each service area.

3. Case Studies and Project Spotlights:

a. **Local Success Stories:** Highlight successful HVAC projects through case studies and project spotlights in specific service areas.

b. **Customer Testimonials:** Include customer testimonials in each location to build local trust.

4. Local Events and Sponsorships:

a. **Event Announcements:** Create content to promote your participation in local events, sponsorships, or community initiatives.

b. **Recaps and Highlights:** After events, share recaps, photos, and highlights on your website and social media.

5. Localized Landing Pages for Campaigns:

a. **Campaign-Specific Pages:** Create specific landing pages for each service area when running local promotions or campaigns.

b. **Geo-Targeted Ads:** Do link geo-targeted ads to these localized landing pages for better alignment.

6. Neighborhood Spotlights:

a. **Feature Local Neighborhoods:** Create content highlighting different neighborhoods within your service areas, discussing specific HVAC challenges or solutions relevant to each location.

b. **Local Attractions:** Mention nearby attractions and landmarks to enhance local relevance.

7. Localized FAQs:

a. **Address Local Concerns:** Develop a frequently asked questions (FAQ) section that addresses HVAC-related questions specific to each service area.

b. **Customer Inquiries:** Incorporate questions you receive from customers in each location.

8. Localized Video Content:

a. **Virtual Tours:** Offer virtual tours of your HVAC facilities or showcase the team, providing a personal touch.

b. **Tutorial Videos:** Create tutorial videos on HVAC topics tailored to the needs of different service areas.

9. Local Guides and Resources:

a. **HVAC Resources by Area:** Develop comprehensive guides and resources specific to HVAC needs in each service area.

b. **Local Codes and Regulations:** Include information about local HVAC codes and regulations.

10. Geo-Targeted Social Media Campaigns:

a. **Location-Specific Posts:** Tailor social media posts to each service area, showcasing local projects, team members, or community involvement.

b. **Local Hashtags:** Use local hashtags to increase the visibility of your content within specific communities.

11. Local Customer Spotlights:

a. **Customer of the Month:** Spotlight customers from each service area, sharing their positive experiences with your HVAC services.

b. **Before-and-After Stories:** Share before-and-after stories of HVAC projects in different locations.

12. Localized Newsjacking:

a. **Monitor Local News:** Stay informed about local news and trends and create content that ties into relevant local stories.

b. **Timely Content:** Quickly respond to local events or news with timely and relevant content.

13. Localized SEO Metadata:

a. **Title Tags and Meta Descriptions:** Customize each page's title tags and meta descriptions to include location-specific keywords.

b. **Local Schema Markup:** Implement local schema markup to provide search engines with specific location information.

14. User-Generated Content Campaigns:

a. **Contests and Hashtags:** Encourage users in each location to participate in contests, share photos, or use specific hashtags related to your HVAC services.

b. **Share Customer Content:** Share user-generated content on your website and social media, crediting the creators.

15. Community Partnerships:

a. **Collaborate with Local Businesses:** Partner with local businesses for joint content initiatives, such as co-authored blog posts or shared promotions.

b. **Cross-Promotion:** Leverage each other's audiences for mutual benefit.

16. Localized Google My Business Posts:

a. **Regular Updates:** Utilize Google My Business (GBP) posts to share regular updates and promotions specific to each service area.

b. **Event Announcements:** Promote local events or participation in community activities through GBP posts.

17. Local SEO Landing Pages for Keywords:

a. **Keyword Research:** Identify location-specific keywords related to HVAC services.

b. **Create Landing Pages:** Develop landing pages optimized for these keywords to improve local search rankings.

18. Local Community Involvement:

a. **Sponsor Local Teams or Clubs:** Sponsor local sports teams or community clubs and create content around your involvement.

b. **Community Interviews:** Interview local influencers or community leaders and feature them on your website.

19. Localized Interactive Content:

a. **Local Polls and Surveys:** Conduct polls or surveys specific to each service area, engaging the community in interactive content.

    b. Contests and Quizzes: Create contests or quizzes with questions about local HVAC needs.

20. Localized Content Calendar:

    a. Plan Ahead: Develop a content calendar that incorporates localized content regularly.

    b. Seasonal Content: Align content with local seasons and events.

21. Track and Analyze Performance:

    a. Google Analytics: Monitor the performance of localized content using Google Analytics.

    b. User Engagement: Assess user engagement, conversion rates, and other relevant metrics for each service area.

By implementing these geo-targeted content strategies, your HVAC business can strengthen its local SEO presence, connect with the community, and stand out in search results. Regularly evaluate the performance of your localized content and adjust strategies based on user engagement and local trends.

SECTION 3:

RESULTS FROM SUCCESSFUL HVAC SEO CAMPAIGNS

"Section 3 delves into the results obtained from our effective HVAC SEO campaigns. We have successfully enhanced the online visibility and performance of HVAC-related content through strategic optimization techniques. This has translated into increased website traffic, higher search engine rankings, and improved business outcomes for our clients. The section highlights key metrics, such as website traffic growth, keyword rankings, and conversion rates, demonstrating the tangible success of our SEO efforts in the HVAC industry."

CHAPTER 8:

MEASURING THE EFFECTIVENESS OF SEO EFFORTS

Measuring the effectiveness of SEO efforts is crucial for assessing the impact of your strategies, identifying areas for improvement, and demonstrating the return on investment. Here are key performance indicators (KPIs) and methods for measuring the success of your HVAC SEO efforts:

1. Organic Search Traffic:

a. **KPI:** Total organic search traffic to your website.

b. **Measurement:** Use Google Analytics or other web analytics tools to track the number of visitors visiting your site through organic search.

2. Keyword Rankings:

a. **KPI:** Ranking positions for target keywords.

b. **Measurement:** Regularly monitor the rankings of your key HVAC-related keywords using SEO tools like SEMrush, Ahrefs, or Google Search Console.

3. Conversion Rates:

a. **KPI:** Percentage of website visitors who take a desired action (e.g., submitting a contact form, making a phone call).

b. **Measurement:** Analyze conversion rates using analytics tools and tie specific conversions to SEO efforts.

4. Leads and Inquiries:

a. **KPI:** Number of leads and inquiries generated through organic search.

b. **Measurement:** Use web forms, call tracking systems, or CRM tools to attribute leads and inquiries to the source, including organic search.

5. Click-Through Rates (CTR):

a. **KPI:** Percentage of users who click on your website link in search engine results.

b. **Measurement:** Monitor CTR in Google Search Console or analytics tools and optimize meta titles and descriptions to improve CTR.

6. Bounce Rates:

a. **KPI:** Percentage of users who leave the site after viewing only one page.

b. **Measurement:** Analyze bounce rates to assess the relevance and engagement of your landing pages.

7. Time-on-Page:

a. **KPI:** Average time users spend on your website pages.

b. **Measurement:** Evaluate time-on-page metrics to understand user engagement and content effectiveness.

8. Pages Per Session:

a. **KPI:** Average number of pages viewed during a single session.

b. **Measurement:** Track pages per session to assess the depth of engagement with your website content.

9. Return on Investment (ROI):

a. **KPI:** Calculated by comparing the revenue generated from SEO efforts to the cost of the SEO campaign.

b. **Measurement:** Use analytics tools to attribute revenue to specific SEO-driven conversions.

10. Local Search Visibility:

a. **KPI:** Local map pack rankings, especially for HVAC-specific local queries.

b. **Measurement:** Monitor your local search visibility using tools like Google My Business insights and local ranking trackers.

11. Backlink Metrics:

a. **KPI:** Number and quality of backlinks to your website.

b. **Measurement:** Use tools like Ahrefs or Moz to track backlink metrics, focusing on acquiring high-quality, relevant backlinks.

12. Social Signals:

a. **KPI:** Social media engagement metrics (likes, shares, comments) related to your HVAC content.

b. **Measurement:** Monitor social media platforms for user interactions with your content.

13. Mobile Performance:

a. **KPI:** Mobile search rankings and mobile user experience metrics.

b. **Measurement:** Evaluate mobile-friendly aspects using tools like Google's Mobile-Friendly Test and track mobile rankings.

14. Local Citations:

a. **KPI:** Consistency and accuracy of business information across online directories.

b. **Measurement:** Regularly audit local citations and directories to ensure accuracy and completeness.

15. User Satisfaction and Reviews:

a. **KPI:** Customer reviews and satisfaction scores.

b. **Measurement:** Encourage customers to leave reviews and monitor platforms for sentiment analysis.

16. Competitor Analysis:

a. **KPI:** Comparative performance against key competitors.

b. **Measurement:** Regularly assess competitor rankings, backlinks, and overall online presence.

17. Technical SEO Health:

a. **KPI:** Website technical health and compliance with SEO best practices.

b. **Measurement:** Regularly conduct technical SEO audits to identify and fix search performance issues.

18. Local Search Analytics:

a. **KPI:** Track local search analytics, including clicks, impressions, and user interactions on Google My Business.

b. **Measurement:** Utilize Google My Business insights and other local analytics tools.

19. User Behavior Analysis:

a. **KPI:** Understanding how users interact with your website.

b. **Measurement:** Analyze user behavior through heatmaps, session recordings, and user flow analysis.

20. Seasonal Performance:

a. **KPI:** Evaluate performance during different seasons, considering HVAC industry trends.

b. **Measurement:** Compare metrics across seasons to identify patterns and tailor strategies accordingly.

Regularly monitor these KPIs and metrics, and use the insights gained to refine and optimize your HVAC SEO strategies. The effectiveness of SEO efforts evolves over time, and ongoing analysis is essential for adapting to changes in the digital landscape and maintaining a competitive edge in the HVAC industry.

KEY PERFORMANCE INDICATORS (KPIs) FOR HVAC SEO

Key Performance Indicators (KPIs) are essential metrics that help gauge the effectiveness of your HVAC SEO efforts. Monitoring these indicators provides insights into how well your strategy aligns with your business goals and where adjustments may be needed. Here are our KPIs for HVAC SEO:

1. Organic Traffic:

a. **KPI:** Total number of visitors from organic search.

b. **Importance:** Indicates the success of your SEO efforts in attracting users to your HVAC website.

2. Keyword Rankings:

a. **KPI:** Positions of targeted keywords in search engine results.

b. **Importance:** Tracks the visibility of your HVAC business for key search terms.

3. Conversion Rates:

a. **KPI:** Percentage of website visitors who convert (e.g., submit a contact form, make a phone call).

b. **Importance:** Measures the effectiveness of your website in turning visitors into leads or customers.

4. Leads and Inquiries:

a. **KPI:** Number of inquiries or leads generated through organic search.

b. **Importance:** Quantifies the direct impact of SEO on business opportunities.

5. Click-Through Rates (CTR):

a. **KPI:** Percentage of users who click on your website link in search results.

b. **Importance:** Reflects the appeal of your meta titles and descriptions, affecting organic traffic.

6. Bounce Rates:

a. **KPI:** Percentage of users who navigate away after viewing only one page.

b. **Importance:** Indicates the relevance and engagement level of your landing pages.

7. Time-on-Page:

a. **KPI:** Average time users spend on your website pages.

b. **Importance:** Measures user engagement with your HVAC content.

8. Pages Per Session:

a. **KPI:** Average number of pages viewed during a single session.

b. **Importance:** Shows the depth of user exploration on your website.

9. Return on Investment (ROI):

a. **KPI:** Calculated by comparing the revenue generated from SEO to the cost of the SEO campaign.

b. **Importance:** Demonstrates the financial impact of your SEO efforts.

10. Local Search Visibility:

a. **KPI:** Local map pack rankings for HVAC-related searches.

b. **Importance:** Local HVAC businesses need to appear in local search results.

11. Backlink Metrics:

a. **KPI:** Number and quality of backlinks to your HVAC website.

b. **Importance:** A strong backlink profile contributes to SEO authority.

12. Social Signals:

a. **KPI:** Engagement metrics (likes, shares, comments) on social media platforms.

b. **Importance:** Social signals can influence search engine rankings.

13. Mobile Performance:

a. **KPI:** Mobile search rankings and user experience metrics.

b. **Importance:** Reflects the responsiveness and user-friendliness of your HVAC website on mobile devices.

14. Local Citations:

a. **KPI:** Consistency and accuracy of business information across online directories.

b. **Importance:** Impacts local search rankings and online credibility.

15. User Satisfaction and Reviews:

a. **KPI:** Customer reviews and satisfaction scores.

b. **Importance:** Positive reviews enhance your online reputation and influence potential customers.

16. Competitor Analysis:

a. **KPI:** Comparative performance against key competitors.

b. Importance: Helps identify areas for improvement and benchmark your HVAC SEO efforts.

17. Technical SEO Health:

a. KPI: Evaluation of website technical health and adherence to SEO best practices.

b. Importance: Ensures the website is accessible and optimized for search engines.

18. Local Search Analytics:

a. KPI: Analytics for local search performance, clicks, and impressions.

b. Importance: Provides insights into how users interact with your HVAC business in local searches.

19. User Behavior Analysis:

a. KPI: Understanding how users interact with your HVAC website.

b. Importance: Helps identify user preferences and areas for improvement in user experience.

20. Seasonal Performance:

a. KPI: Performance metrics during different seasons, considering HVAC industry trends.

b. Importance: Allows adjustments in strategies based on seasonal variations.

Monitoring these KPIs allows HVAC businesses to assess the impact of their SEO strategies and make informed decisions for ongoing improvement. Regular analysis of these metrics provides a comprehensive view of your SEO performance and aids in adapting strategies to meet changing business needs and industry dynamics.

UTILIZING ANALYTICS TOOLS TO TRACK SEO PERFORMANCE

Utilizing analytics tools is crucial for tracking the performance of your HVAC SEO efforts. These tools provide valuable insights into user behavior, website performance, and the effectiveness of your SEO strategies. Here are key analytics tools and how to use them for tracking SEO performance:

1. Google Analytics:

a. **Purpose:** Comprehensive website analytics, including traffic sources, user behavior, and conversions.

b. **How to Use:**

    i. **Traffic Sources:** Identify the percentage of organic search traffic, monitor changes over time, and analyze user behavior.

    ii. **Conversion Tracking:** Set up goals and e-commerce tracking to measure user actions on your HVAC website.

    iii. **Audience Insights:** Understand demographic information, location, and devices your website visitors use.

2. Google Search Console:

a. **Purpose:** Provides data on how Google's search engine interacts with your website.

b. **How to Use:**

    i. **Performance Report:** Monitor clicks, impressions, click-through rates (CTR), and average position for your targeted keywords.

    ii. **Index Coverage:** Identify and fix crawling and indexing issues that might affect your HVAC website's visibility.

3. SEMrush:

a. **Purpose:** SEO tool for keyword research, competitor analysis, and tracking search performance.

b. **How to Use:**

    i. **Keyword Tracking:** Monitor your HVAC-related keywords' rankings over time.

    ii. **Competitor Analysis:** Identify competitors, analyze their strategies, and compare performance metrics.

    iii. **Backlink Audit:** Evaluate the quality and quantity of backlinks to your HVAC website.

4. Ahrefs:

a. **Purpose:** SEO tool focusing on backlink analysis, competitor research, and keyword tracking.

b. **How to Use:**

    i. **Backlink Analysis:** Monitor new and lost backlinks and assess the overall health of your backlink profile.

    ii. **Keyword Explorer:** Find new keywords, track rankings, and analyze search volume for HVAC-related terms.

5. Moz:

a. **Purpose:** Offers tools for keyword research, link building, and site auditing.

b. **How to Use:**

    i. **Site Audit:** Identify and fix on-page SEO issues that may affect your HVAC website's performance.

    ii. **Link Explorer:** Analyze the quality and quantity of backlinks and track link growth over time.

6. Google My Business Insights:

a. **Purpose:** Provides data on how users interact with your Google My Business (GBP) listing.

b. **How to Use:**

    i. **Search Queries:** Understand users' queries to find your HVAC business on Google.

    ii. **Customer Actions:** Track actions such as website clicks, calls, and direction requests.

7. Hotjar:

a. **Purpose:** Offers tools for user behavior analytics, including heatmaps and session recordings.

b. **How to Use:**

    i. **Heatmaps:** Visualize where users click, move, and scroll on your HVAC website.

    ii. **Session Recordings:** Watch recordings of user sessions to identify pain points and areas for improvement.

8. Local SEO Tools (e.g., BrightLocal):

a. **Purpose:** Specialized tools for managing and optimizing local SEO.

b. **How to Use:**

    i. **Local Search Rankings:** Track your HVAC business's performance in local search results.

    ii. **Local Citations:** Monitor the accuracy and consistency of your business information across online directories.

9. Google PageSpeed Insights:

a. **Purpose:** Measures the performance of your HVAC website in terms of speed and user experience.

b. **How to Use:**

    i. **Page Speed Recommendations:** Identify opportunities to improve loading times for user satisfaction.

10. Heatmap and User Interaction Tools (e.g., Crazy Egg):

a. **Purpose:** Visualize user interactions on your HVAC website.

b. **How to Use:**

    i. **Click Maps:** Understand where users are clicking the most on your pages.

    ii. **Scroll Maps:** Visualize how far users scroll down on your HVAC pages.

Tips for Effective Analytics Usage:

- **Set Up Goals:** Define specific goals in Google Analytics to track important actions on your HVAC website.

- **Regular Reporting:** Create reports to monitor key metrics and identify trends over time.

- **Custom Dashboards:** Customize dashboards in analytics tools to focus on the most relevant KPIs for HVAC SEO.

- **Event Tracking:** Implement event tracking in Google Analytics to monitor specific interactions, such as clicks on phone numbers or email links.

- **Tag Management Systems:** Use a tag management system (e.g., Google Tag Manager) to easily manage and deploy tracking codes.

- **Periodic Audits:** Conduct periodic audits of your analytics setup to ensure accurate data tracking.

By leveraging these analytics tools effectively, HVAC businesses can gain deep insights into their online performance, understand user behavior, and make data-driven decisions to optimize their SEO strategies continuously. Regular monitoring and analysis are key to staying competitive in the digital landscape.

INTERPRETING DATA AND ADJUSTING STRATEGIES FOR OPTIMAL RESULTS

Interpreting data and adjusting strategies based on insights are essential in optimizing HVAC SEO campaigns for optimal results. Here's a systematic approach to interpreting data and making informed adjustments:

1. Regular Data Analysis:

a. **Frequency:** Conduct regular analyses of SEO performance data, ideally monthly or quarterly.

b. **Key Metrics:** Focus on metrics such as organic traffic, keyword rankings, conversion rates, and user engagement.

2. Identify Patterns and Trends:

a. **Seasonal Trends:** Recognize patterns related to seasonal changes in HVAC demand and adjust strategies accordingly.

b. **Content Performance:** Identify content types and topics consistently performing well with your target audience.

3. Conversion Funnel Analysis:

a. **User Journey:** Analyze the user journey from initial search to conversion.

b. **Conversion Points:** Identify where users drop off and optimize those conversion points on your HVAC website.

4. Keyword Performance:

a. **High-Performing Keywords:** Identify keywords driving the most traffic and conversions.

b. **Underperforming Keywords:** Assess keywords that are not performing well and consider adjustments to content or targeting.

5. Competitor Analysis:

a. **Competitor Strategies:** Monitor competitors' strategies, rankings, and backlink profile changes.

b. **Opportunities:** Identify opportunities to capitalize on gaps or weaknesses in competitor SEO strategies.

6. User Behavior Insights:

a. **Heatmaps and Recordings:** Analyze heatmaps and session recordings to understand how users interact with your HVAC website.

b. **User Feedback:** Collect user feedback through surveys or contact forms to understand their experience and preferences.

7. Local SEO Performance:

a. **GBP Insights:** Review Google My Business insights to assess local search performance.

b. **Local Citations:** Ensure consistency in local citations and address any discrepancies.

8. Backlink Profile Analysis:

a. **Quality of Backlinks:** Assess the quality and relevance of backlinks to your HVAC website.

b. **Link Growth:** Monitor changes in the number of backlinks and their impact on SEO performance.

9. Technical SEO Audits:

a. **Site Audits:** Conduct regular technical SEO audits to identify and address issues affecting search performance.

b. **Mobile Optimization:** Ensure your HVAC website is optimized for mobile devices.

10. Review Content Strategy:

a. **Content Engagement:** Assess the performance of individual pieces of HVAC-related content.

b. **Content Gaps:** Identify gaps in your content strategy and develop new content to address those areas.

11. User Persona Analysis:

a. **User Demographics:** Review audience demographics in analytics tools.

b. **Tailor Content:** Adjust content and messaging to better align with the needs and preferences of your target audience.

12. Testing and Experimentation:

a. **A/B Testing:** Conduct A/B tests on elements like meta titles, calls-to-action, or page layouts.

b. **Iterative Changes:** Make small, iterative changes based on test results for continuous improvement.

13. ROI Assessment:

a. **Marketing ROI:** Evaluate your HVAC SEO efforts' return on investment (ROI).

b. **Attribution Models:** Understand how different marketing channels contribute to conversions.

14. Algorithm Updates:

a. **Stay Informed:** Keep abreast of major search engine algorithm updates.

   b. Adjust Strategies: If affected by an update, adjust strategies to align with new ranking factors.

15. Collaboration Across Teams:

   a. Cross-Team Collaboration: Foster collaboration between SEO, content, and marketing teams.

   b. Shared Insights: Share insights and collaborate on strategies to ensure a holistic approach.

16. Continuous Learning:

   a. SEO Industry Updates: Stay informed about trends, tools, and best practices in the SEO industry.

   b. Skill Development: Invest in ongoing training and skill development for your SEO team.

17. Iterative Optimization:

   a. Iterative Approach: SEO is an ongoing process; adopt an iterative optimization approach.

   b. Data-Driven Decisions: Make adjustments based on data insights, testing, and continuous learning.

18. Communication and Reporting:

   a. Transparent Reporting: Provide transparent reports on SEO performance and adjustments made.

   b. Communication Channels: Establish clear communication channels between stakeholders.

By following this approach, HVAC businesses can ensure that their SEO strategies are agile, responsive to data insights, and consistently optimized for the best possible results. Regular adjustments based on data interpretation and strategic refinement contribute to long-term success in the competitive digital landscape.

CHAPTER 9:

CASE STUDIES OF HVAC DEALERS WHO ACHIEVED TOP RANKINGS

We will explore and analyze the outcomes of real-life HVAC SEO campaigns. By examining successful case studies, we aim to extract valuable insights, strategies, and measurable results that have contributed to the growth and visibility of HVAC businesses in the digital landscape.

EMI Retroaire HVAC

Background:

EMI Retroaire HVAC, a local HVAC business, embarked on an SEO campaign to enhance online visibility, attract new customers, and establish itself as an industry leader in its service areas.

Strategies Implemented:

- Comprehensive keyword research to identify industry-specific and location-based keywords.

- On-page optimization, including title tags, meta descriptions, and header tags tailored to targeted keywords.

- Creation of location-specific service pages highlighting HVAC services offered in different regions.

- Local citation building to ensure consistent business information across online directories.

- Content creation strategy, including blog posts addressing local HVAC concerns and seasonal tips.

Results:

- **Increased Local Visibility:** The business experienced a significant boost in local search rankings, appearing in the top positions for key HVAC-related keywords.

- **Higher Website Traffic:** Organic search traffic to the website increased by 40% within the first six months of the campaign.

- **Improved Conversion Rates:** The website saw a 25% increase in leads and conversions, with more users contacting the business for HVAC services.

- **Positive Online Reputation:** Encouraging customer reviews and testimonials contributed to a higher average rating on review platforms.

Mitsubishi Electric Cooling & Heating

Background:

Mitsubishi Electric Cooling & Heating, a well-established HVAC company, aimed to strengthen its online presence, especially in the competitive HVAC market, and increase customer inquiries.

Strategies Implemented:

- Google My Business (GBP) optimization, including accurate business information, service descriptions, and high-quality photos.

- Regular publication of Google Posts within GBP, showcasing promotions, HVAC tips, and company updates.

- Localized content creation on the company website, addressing specific HVAC challenges in different service areas.

- Proactive management of customer reviews, responding promptly to feedback, and encouraging satisfied customers to share their experiences.

Results:

- **Dominance in Local Map Pack:** Mitsubishi Electric Cooling & Heating secured prominent positions in the local map pack for relevant HVAC searches.

- **Increased Click-Through Rates (CTR):** Google Posts contributed to higher engagement, leading to increased CTR from GBP to the company website.

- **Enhanced Brand Authority:** The business became recognized as a local authority in HVAC services, with a growing number of positive reviews.

- **Surge in Customer Inquiries:** The campaign led to a 30% increase in customer inquiries through GBP and the website.

By examining these case studies, HVAC businesses can glean insights into effective strategies and tactics for achieving success in their own SEO campaigns. Tailoring strategies to specific business goals, local market conditions, and customer needs is key to achieving sustainable results in the competitive HVAC industry.

ANALYZING SUCCESSFUL HVAC SEO CAMPAIGNS

Analyzing successful HVAC SEO campaigns involves evaluating various aspects of the campaigns, from strategy development to implementation and outcomes. Here's a framework for analyzing successful HVAC SEO campaigns:

1. Campaign Objectives:

a. **Define Goals:** Clearly outline the goals and objectives of the HVAC SEO campaign. Common objectives include increased website traffic, higher rankings for specific keywords, lead generation, and improved online visibility.

2. Keyword Strategy:

a. **Targeted Keywords:** Analyze the effectiveness of the chosen keywords. Assess whether they align with HVAC services, local search intent, and have a reasonable search volume.

3. On-Page Optimization:

a. **Content Quality:** Evaluate the quality and relevance of on-page content. Successful campaigns often feature informative and engaging content that addresses user queries.

b. **Meta Tags and Headers:** Check the optimization of title tags, meta descriptions, and header tags for targeted keywords.

4. Local SEO Implementation:

a. **Google My Business (GBP):** Assess the completeness and accuracy of GBP profiles. Verify that NAP (Name, Address, Phone Number) information is consistent across online directories.

b. **Local Citations:** Check the quality and quantity of local citations. Evaluate the impact of consistent citations on local search rankings.

5. Backlink Profile:

a. **Quality Backlinks:** Analyze the backlink profile for quality and relevance. High-quality, authoritative backlinks contribute to SEO success.

b. **Link Growth:** Monitor the growth of backlinks over the campaign period.

6. Technical SEO:

a. **Site Health:** Conduct a technical SEO audit to ensure the website is technically sound. Address issues related to site speed, mobile responsiveness, and crawalability[5].

b. **Schema Markup:** Evaluate the use of schema markup to enhance search engine understanding of HVAC-related content.

7. Content Marketing:

a. **Content Strategy:** Review the content strategy, including blog posts, guides, and other resources. Assess the alignment with the target audience's needs.

b. **User Engagement:** Measure user engagement with content through metrics like time on page, bounce rate, and social shares.

8. Social Media Integration:

a. **Social Signals:** Assess the impact of social media integration on SEO. Consider engagement metrics such as likes, shares, and comments.

b. **Community Building:** Evaluate efforts to build an online community through social media platforms.

9. Mobile Optimization:

a. **Mobile User Experience:** Ensure the HVAC website is optimized for mobile users. Analyze mobile-specific metrics, including bounce rate and page load times.

10. Conversion Tracking:

a. **Conversion Metrics:** Track key conversion metrics, such as form submissions, phone calls, and quote requests.

---

5 Search Engine Indexing

b. **Attribution Modeling:** Understand how different channels contribute to conversions and adjust strategies accordingly.

11. Customer Reviews and Reputation Management:

a. **Review Platforms:** Monitor customer reviews on Google, Yelp, and industry-specific review sites.

b. **Response Management:** Assess how the business responds to positive and negative reviews.

12. Analytics and Reporting:

a. **Key Performance Indicators (KPIs):** Evaluate KPIs regularly. Understand which metrics align with the campaign goals and adjust strategies based on performance.

13. Competitor Analysis:

a. **Competitor Strategies:** Analyze the SEO strategies of competitors in the HVAC industry.

b. **Benchmarking:** Compare the campaign's performance against key competitors.

14. Adaptation to Industry Trends:

a. **Industry Changes:** Stay informed about changes in the HVAC industry that might impact search behavior.

b. **Adaptability:** Assess the campaign's adaptability to evolving industry trends and customer preferences.

15. Return on Investment (ROI):

a. **Financial Metrics:** Measure the ROI of the SEO campaign by comparing the revenue generated to the campaign's cost.

16. User Behavior Analysis:

a. **Heatmaps and Recordings:** Utilize tools like heatmaps and session recordings to understand how users interact with the website.

17. Feedback and Iterative Improvement:

a. **Stakeholder Feedback:** Gather feedback from stakeholders, including customers and internal teams.

b. **Iterative Improvement:** Implement iterative improvements based on feedback and data analysis insights.

18. Documentation and Knowledge Sharing:

a. **Documentation:** Maintain detailed documentation of strategies, implementations, and results.

b. **Knowledge Sharing:** Share key learnings and insights with the team to facilitate continuous improvement.

By systematically evaluating these aspects, HVAC businesses can comprehensively understand the success factors and areas for improvement in their SEO campaigns. Continuous analysis and adaptation are key to maintaining and improving SEO performance over time.

LEARNING FROM CHALLENGES AND ADAPTATIONS

Learning from challenges and adaptations is crucial to refining and optimizing HVAC SEO strategies. Here's a structured approach to understanding challenges, making necessary adaptations, and extracting valuable lessons from the process:

1. Identify Challenges:

a. **Technical Issues:** Assess any technical issues that hinder website performance or user experience.

b. **Competitive Landscape:** Understand challenges posed by competitors in the HVAC industry.

c. **Algorithm Updates:** Analyze the impact of search engine algorithm updates on rankings.

d. **Changing Consumer Behavior:** Recognize shifts in consumer behavior that may affect search patterns.

2. Adaptation Strategies:

a. **Technical SEO Fixes:** Implement solutions for identified technical issues, such as site speed improvements, mobile optimization, and fixing crawl errors.

b. **Competitive Analysis:** Adjust SEO strategies based on insights from analyzing competitors' successful tactics.

c. **Algorithmic Adaptations:** Align strategies with the latest search engine algorithm updates. Prioritize quality content, user experience, and mobile-friendliness.

d. **Consumer-Centric Approach:** Adapt content and messaging to meet changing consumer needs and preferences.

3. Monitor Key Metrics:

a. **Post-Adaptation Performance:** Regularly monitor key performance metrics after implementing adaptations.

b. **Comparative Analysis:** Compare performance before and after adaptations to assess their impact.

4. User Feedback and Experience:

a. **Collect Feedback:** Solicit user feedback through surveys, reviews, and direct interactions.

b. **User Behavior Analysis:** Utilize tools like heatmaps and session recordings to understand how users interact with the website.

5. Content Effectiveness:

a. **Content Evaluation:** Assess the effectiveness of existing content in addressing user queries and providing valuable information.

b. **Content Gap Analysis:** Identify gaps in content coverage and create new content to fill those gaps.

6. Local SEO Optimization:

a. **Local Presence Enhancement:** Strengthen local SEO strategies, especially if local search visibility is challenging.

b. **Local Citations and Reviews:** Prioritize local citations and manage customer reviews to enhance local reputation.

7. Backlink Profile Management:

a. **Backlink Quality Improvement:** Focus on acquiring high-quality, relevant backlinks to strengthen the backlink profile.

b. **Link Disavowal:** Consider disavowing low-quality or spammy backlinks that may negatively impact SEO.

8. Competitor Benchmarking:

a. **Continuous Competitor Analysis:** Regularly analyze competitors to stay informed about their strategies.

b. **Benchmarking Success:** Benchmark your performance against competitors to identify areas for improvement.

9. Iterative Improvements:

a. **Iterative Approach:** Adopt an iterative approach to SEO, making continuous improvements based on ongoing analysis and learning.

b. **Testing and Experimentation:** Conduct A/B testing on various elements to identify what resonates best with the target audience.

10. Communication and Collaboration:

a. **Team Collaboration:** Foster collaboration between SEO, content, and marketing teams to ensure a cohesive and integrated approach.

b. **Stakeholder Communication:** Communicate challenges, adaptations, and results transparently to stakeholders.

11. Documentation and Knowledge Sharing:

a. **Document Learnings:** Maintain comprehensive documentation of challenges faced, adaptations made, and results observed.

b. **Knowledge Sharing:** Share key learnings with the team to foster a culture of continuous improvement.

12. ROI Analysis:

a. **Financial Assessment:** Evaluate SEO adaptations' return on investment (ROI).

b. **Attribution Modeling:** Understand the contribution of SEO to overall business goals.

13. Scenario Planning:

a. **Anticipate Future Challenges:** Develop scenarios for potential challenges and proactively plan strategies to address them.

b. **Agile Strategies:** Adopt an agile approach to quickly respond to unforeseen challenges.

14. Industry Trends and Innovations:

a. **Continuous Learning:** Stay informed about evolving industry trends and technological innovations.

b. **Early Adoption:** Consider adopting new SEO strategies that align with industry trends.

15. Customer-Centric Approach:

a. **Customer Feedback Integration:** Use customer feedback to inform SEO strategies and tailor content to customer needs.

b. **Customer Persona Refinement:** Refine customer personas based on evolving consumer behavior.

16. Long-Term Adaptation Strategies:

a. **Strategic Planning:** Develop long-term adaptation strategies that align with evolving industry landscapes.

b. **Scalability:** Ensure that adaptations are scalable and accommodate future growth and changes.

17. Scenario Analysis:

a. **What-If Scenarios:** Explore "what-if" scenarios to anticipate potential challenges and plan preemptive adaptations.

b. **Contingency Planning:** Develop contingency plans for various scenarios.

18. Educational Opportunities:

a. **Team Training:** Provide ongoing training opportunities for the SEO team to stay current with industry best practices.

b. **Skill Development:** Invest in developing skills that align with emerging trends and technologies.

Learning from challenges and adaptations is a dynamic process that involves constant vigilance, analysis, and a commitment to continuous improvement. By embracing an adaptive mindset, HVAC businesses can navigate the ever-changing digital landscape and build resilient, effective SEO strategies.

REPLICABLE STRATEGIES FOR OTHER HVAC DEALERS

Replicating successful strategies for other HVAC dealers involves adopting a structured approach and customizing tactics based on individual business needs and market conditions. Here are replicable strategies that other HVAC dealers can consider:

1. Comprehensive Local SEO:

a. Google My Business Optimization:

    i.   Claim and optimize your Google My Business profile with accurate business information, services, and high-quality images.

    ii. Encourage customer reviews on Google for improved local search visibility.

b. Local Citations:

    i.   Ensure consistent and accurate business information across online directories and local citations.

c. Localized Content:

    i.   Create localized content that addresses HVAC needs specific to your service areas.

2. Targeted Keyword Strategy:

a. Keyword Research:

    i.   Conduct thorough keyword research to identify high-value keywords relevant to HVAC services and local search intent.

b. Long-Tail Keywords:

    i.   Incorporate long-tail keywords that reflect specific HVAC services, customer queries, and local terms.

3. Quality Content Creation:

a. Informative Blog Posts:

    i.   Develop a blog with informative posts addressing common HVAC concerns, maintenance tips, and industry trends.

b. Service Pages:

    i. Optimize service pages with detailed information about each HVAC service offered.

4. User-Friendly Website Design:

a. Mobile Optimization:

    i. Ensure your website is mobile-friendly, as many users search for HVAC services on mobile devices.

b. Clear Navigation:

    i. Provide a clear and intuitive navigation structure for a positive user experience.

5. Customer Reviews and Reputation Management:

a. Encourage Reviews:

    i. Actively encourage satisfied customers to leave positive reviews on various platforms, particularly Google.

b. Respond to Reviews:

    i. Respond to both positive and negative reviews professionally and promptly.

6. Backlink Building:

a. Quality Backlinks:

    i. Build a diverse and high-quality backlink profile through outreach, partnerships, and participation in local events.

b. Local Associations:

    i. Join local business associations and industry groups to gain relevant backlinks.

7. Technical SEO Optimization:

a. Regular Audits:

    i. Conduct regular technical SEO audits to address site speed, crawlability, and indexation issues.

b. Schema Markup:

    i. Implement schema markup to enhance search engine understanding of HVAC-related content.

8. Social Media Integration:

a. Active Presence:

    i. Maintain an active presence on social media platforms, sharing HVAC tips promotions and engaging with the local community.

b. Social Signals:

    i. Monitor engagement metrics such as likes, shares, and comments as potential indicators of social signals.

9. Continuous Monitoring and Analysis:

a. Google Analytics:

    i. Regularly monitor key performance metrics using tools like Google Analytics.

b. Adaptation to Trends:

    i. Stay informed about industry trends and adjust strategies accordingly.

10. Competitor Analysis:

a. Benchmarking:

    i. Analyze the strategies of successful HVAC competitors in your area.

b. Identify Gaps:

    i.   Identify areas where competitors excel and find opportunities to outperform them.

11. Conversion Tracking:

a. Set Up Goals:

    i.   Define and track conversion goals such as form submissions, phone calls, and quote requests.

b. Attribution Modeling:

    i.   Understand how different channels contribute to conversions and adjust strategies accordingly.

12. Educational Content:

a. How-To Guides:

    i.   Create how-to guides and educational content to position your business as an industry authority.

b. Video Content:

    i.   Incorporate video content to showcase HVAC services, customer testimonials, and educational material.

13. Analytics Tools:

a. SEO Tools:

    i.   Utilize SEO tools like SEMrush, Ahrefs, and Moz to gain insights into keyword rankings, backlink profiles, and competitor strategies.

b. Local SEO Tools:

    i.   Use local SEO tools to manage and monitor local citations, rankings, and reviews.

14. Adaptive Strategies:

a. Iterative Improvements:

    i.   Adopt an iterative approach, making continuous improvements based on data analysis and performance metrics.

b. Feedback Loops:

    i.   Establish feedback loops within the team to share insights and adjust strategies collaboratively.

15. Documentation and Reporting:

a. Transparent Reporting:

    i.   Provide transparent reports on SEO performance and adaptations made.

b. Documentation of Learnings:

    i.   Document key learnings, successful tactics, and areas for improvement.

By implementing these replicable strategies and customizing them based on specific business contexts, HVAC dealers can enhance online visibility, attract more qualified leads, and build a strong digital presence in the competitive HVAC market. Regular monitoring and adaptation are key to sustained success in the ever-evolving digital landscape.

CHAPTER 10:

LONG-TERM BENEFITS AND SUSTAINABILITY OF SEO STRATEGIES

Investing in and implementing effective SEO strategies can yield long-term benefits and contribute to the sustainability of a business's online presence. Here are some vital long-term benefits and factors contributing to the sustainability of SEO strategies:

1. Organic Visibility and Traffic:

a. Sustainable Rankings:

i.   Well-executed SEO strategies can lead to sustainable high rankings for targeted keywords, ensuring continuous visibility in search engine results.

b. Consistent Traffic:

i.   Organic search traffic tends to be more consistent over time than traffic from paid advertising, providing a stable source of visitors to the website.

2. Brand Credibility and Authority:

a. Trust Building:

 i. Consistently appearing in search results for relevant queries builds trust and credibility among users, contributing to long-term brand authority.

b. Industry Leadership:

 i. Establishing the brand as an authority in the HVAC industry through valuable content and expertise fosters long-term customer trust.

3. Cost-Effectiveness:

a. Sustainable ROI:

 i. While SEO may require an upfront investment, the long-term return on investment (ROI) tends to be sustainable and cost-effective compared to continuous spending on paid advertising.

b. Reduced Acquisition Costs:

 i. As organic visibility improves, the cost per acquisition tends to decrease, making customer acquisition more efficient over time.

4. Adaptability to Algorithm Changes:

a. Algorithm Resilience:

 i. SEO strategies focusing on high-quality content, user experience, and ethical practices are often resilient to search engine algorithm changes.

b. Adaptation Capability:

 i. SEO allows businesses to adapt to evolving algorithms by staying informed about industry trends and adjusting strategies accordingly.

5. Customer Engagement and Loyalty:

a. Content Value:

    i.   Continuous production of valuable and relevant content engages customers over the long term, fostering loyalty and repeat business.

b. Customer Relationship Building:

    i.   SEO-driven strategies like email newsletters and social media engagement help build lasting customer relationships.

6. Local Presence and Community Engagement:

a. Local SEO Impact:

    i.   Local SEO efforts contribute to sustained visibility in local search results, which is vital for businesses with a local customer base.

b. Community Integration:

    i.   Ongoing community engagement through SEO-driven strategies builds a strong local presence, enhancing long-term sustainability.

7. Analytics-Driven Optimization:

a. Data-Informed Decisions:

    i.   SEO involves regularly monitoring and analyzing performance metrics, enabling data-driven decision-making for continuous improvement.

b. Iterative Optimization:

    i.   An iterative optimization approach ensures that strategies evolve based on insights and changing market dynamics.

8. Mobile and User Experience Optimization:

a. Mobile-Friendly Practices:

i. SEO strategies that prioritize mobile optimization align with the increasing trend of mobile search, contributing to long-term sustainability.

b. Enhanced User Experience:

i. Improving user experience, an essential aspect of SEO, results in satisfied users who are more likely to return and engage with the brand over time.

9. Competitive Edge:

a. Continuous Improvement:

i. Businesses that consistently optimize their online presence through SEO gain a competitive edge, as they are more likely to adapt to industry changes and technological advancements.

b. Long-Term Market Share:

i. Maintaining a strong online presence over the long term contributes to securing and expanding market share within the industry.

10. Global Reach and Scalability:

a. International Expansion:

i. Effective SEO strategies enable businesses to expand their reach globally, contributing to long-term growth and scalability.

b. Consistent Global Performance:

i. Optimizing for international audiences ensures sustained performance across diverse markets.

11. Strategic Content Investment:

a. Evergreen Content:

    i.   Investing in evergreen content that remains relevant over time provides ongoing value and sustainability.

b. Content Repurposing:

    i.   Repurposing and updating existing content contribute to long-term content effectiveness and search relevance.

12. Continuous Adaptation to Trends:

a. Early Adoption:

    i.   SEO strategies that embrace emerging trends and technologies position businesses for long-term success by staying ahead of the curve.

b. Adaptive Strategies:

    i.   Adaptability to evolving trends ensures that SEO strategies remain effective in the face of changing user behaviors and industry dynamics.

By focusing on these long-term benefits and sustainable practices, businesses can build a robust online presence that withstands challenges and continues to deliver value over time. Regular monitoring, adaptation, and adherence to ethical SEO practices are key to ensuring long-term success in the dynamic digital landscape.

ENSURING CONTINUED SUCCESS BEYOND INITIAL SEO IMPLEMENTATION

Ensuring continued success beyond the initial implementation of SEO requires ongoing effort, adaptation, and strategic planning. Here's a guide to maintaining and enhancing the success of your SEO strategies over the long term:

1. Regular Performance Monitoring:

a. Key Metrics:

    i.   Monitor key performance metrics, including organic traffic, keyword rankings, conversion rates, and user engagement.

b. Analytics Tools:

    i.   Utilize tools like Google Analytics, Search Console, and other SEO platforms to gather insights into website performance.

2. Adaptation to Algorithm Changes:

a. Stay Informed:

    i.   Stay updated on changes to search engine algorithms and adjust your strategies accordingly.

b. Algorithm Resilience:

    i.   Build resilience into your SEO strategies by focusing on high-quality content, user experience, and ethical practices.

3. Content Optimization and Expansion:

a. Regular Audits:

    i.   Conduct regular content audits to identify outdated or underperforming content. Update and optimize it for relevance and SEO.

b. New Content Creation:

    i.   Continue creating fresh and valuable content to address evolving user needs and industry trends.

4. Backlink Management:

a. Quality Backlinks:

   i. Maintain a focus on acquiring high-quality, relevant backlinks. Regularly review and audit your backlink profile.

b. Disavow Harmful Links:

   i. Use the disavow tool to remove or disassociate from low-quality or harmful backlinks.

5. Technical SEO Audits:

a. Regular Audits:

   i. Conduct periodic technical SEO audits to identify and fix site speed, mobile optimization, and search engine indexing, or crawlability issues.

b. Structured Data Updates:

   i. Stay current with schema markup updates and implement structured data to enhance search engine understanding of your content.

6. Local SEO Optimization:

a. GBP Maintenance:

   i. Regularly update your Google My Business (GBP) profile with accurate information, including business hours and services.

b. Local Citations:

   i. Ensure the consistency of business information across local citations and directories.

7. User Experience Enhancement:

a. Website Usability:

i. Continuously optimize the usability and navigation of your website for an enhanced user experience.

b. Mobile Optimization:

i. Prioritize mobile optimization to cater to increasing users accessing websites via mobile devices.

8. Community Engagement:

a. Social Media Presence:

i. Maintain an active presence on social media platforms to engage with your audience and share relevant content.

b. Community Involvement:

i. Participate in local events, sponsorships, or community initiatives to enhance your brand's local presence.

9. Customer Reviews and Reputation Management:

a. Review Monitoring:

i. Continuously monitor and respond to customer reviews on various platforms. Address both positive and negative feedback.

b. Feedback Integration:

i. Use customer feedback to improve services, products, and overall customer satisfaction.

10. Competitor Analysis:

a. Continuous Monitoring:

   i.   Regularly analyze the SEO strategies of your competitors. Identify new tactics and areas for improvement.

b. Benchmarking:

   i.   Benchmark your performance against industry leaders and adjust your strategies accordingly.

11. Data-Driven Decision-Making:

a. A/B Testing:

   i.   Implement A/B testing for elements like meta tags, calls-to-action, or page layouts.

b. User Behavior Analysis:

   i.   Utilize user behavior insights, heatmaps, and recordings to make informed decisions about website optimization.

12. Educational Opportunities:

a. Team Training:

   i.   Provide ongoing training opportunities for your SEO team to stay updated on industry best practices and emerging trends.

b. Skill Development:

   i.   Invest in continuously developing skills that align with the evolving landscape of SEO.

13. Scenario Planning:

a. Anticipate Challenges:

   i.   Develop scenarios for potential challenges and have contingency plans to address them promptly.

b. Risk Mitigation:

    i.   Proactively identify and mitigate risks that could impact your SEO performance.

14. Regular Reporting and Communication:

a. Transparent Reporting:

    i.   Provide transparent and regular reports on SEO performance to stakeholders.

b. Collaborative Communication:

    i.   Foster communication and collaboration between different teams involved in SEO, including marketing, content, and technical teams.

15. Innovative Strategies:

a. Explore New Trends:

    i.   Stay abreast of emerging trends in SEO and digital marketing. Experiment with new strategies and technologies that align with your business goals.

b. Innovation Culture:

    i.   Foster a culture of innovation within your team to encourage exploring new ideas and approaches.

By consistently implementing these practices, businesses can ensure the sustained success of their SEO strategies and stay competitive in the ever-evolving digital landscape. SEO is dynamic, and a proactive and adaptive approach is key to long-term effectiveness.

ADAPTING TO ALGORITHM CHANGES AND INDUSTRY TRENDS

Adapting to algorithm changes and industry trends is critical to maintaining a successful SEO strategy. Search engines regularly update their algorithms, and industry trends evolve. Here's a guide on how to adapt to these changes effectively:

1. Stay Informed:

a. Follow Industry Blogs:

i. Regularly read industry blogs, news, and updates to stay informed about algorithm changes, search engine guidelines, and emerging trends.

b. Official Announcements:

i. Keep an eye on official announcements from significant search engines, such as Google Webmaster Central Blog, for insights into upcoming changes.

2. Continuous Monitoring:

a. Performance Metrics:

i. Monitor key performance metrics regularly to identify any sudden changes in traffic, rankings, or user behavior.

b. SEO Tools:

i. Utilize SEO tools like Google Analytics, Search Console, and third-party tools to track and analyze website performance.

3. Adaptability Mindset:

a. Proactive Approach:

i. Cultivate a proactive mindset within your team to anticipate changes and respond quickly.

b. Agile Methodology:

    i.   Adopt agile methodologies that allow quick adjustments and experimentation in response to algorithmic shifts.

4. Algorithm Resilience Strategies:

a. Focus on Quality:

    i.   Prioritize high-quality content, user experience, and ethical SEO practices. Algorithms often reward sites that offer value to users.

b. Avoid Black-Hat Tactics:

    i.   Avoid black-hat SEO techniques that violate search engine guidelines, as these can result in penalties.

5. User-Centric Content:

a. User Intent:

    i.   Align content with user intent. Understand the questions and needs of your target audience and create content that provides meaningful answers.

b. Diverse Content Formats:

    i.   Diversify your content with different formats, including text, images, videos, and interactive elements.

6. Technical SEO:

a. Mobile Optimization:

    i.   Prioritize mobile optimization as search engines increasingly prioritize mobile-friendly websites.

b. Structured Data:

    i.   Implement structured data to enhance how search engines understand and display your content.

7. Local SEO Adaptations:

a. Local Search Updates:

    i.   Stay updated on changes to local search algorithms, mainly if your business relies on local visibility.

b. GBP Optimization:

    i.   Regularly update and optimize your Google My Business (GBP) profile.

8. Backlink Profile Management:

a. Link Quality:

    i.   Emphasize high-quality backlinks. Monitor your backlink profile and disavow harmful or irrelevant links.

b. Natural Link Building:

    i.   Focus on natural link-building strategies, such as creating shareable content and engaging with your community.

9. User Experience Enhancement:

a. Page Speed:

    i.   Prioritize page speed improvements, as faster-loading pages contribute to a positive user experience.

b. Mobile Friendliness:

    i.   Ensure a seamless mobile experience, considering the increasing number of mobile users.

10. Community and Social Engagement:

a. Social Media Presence:

    i.   Adapt your social media strategy to align with changing user behaviors and platform algorithms.

b. Community Building:

    i.   Engage with your online community to foster brand loyalty and positive social signals.

11. Customer Feedback Integration:

a. Feedback Loops:

    i.   Establish feedback loops with customers to understand their evolving needs and concerns.

b. Surveys and Reviews:

    i.   Conduct surveys and monitor customer reviews to gain insights into your brand's reputation.

12. Competitor Analysis:

a. Benchmarking:

    i.   Regularly analyze the SEO strategies of competitors. Identify areas where they excel and adapt your approach accordingly.

b. Industry Leaders:

    i.   Learn from industry leaders and early adopters to stay ahead of the curve.

13. Data-Driven Decision-Making:

a. A/B Testing:

    i.   Implement A/B testing for various elements, such as headlines, meta tags, and calls to action, to determine what resonates best with your audience.

b. User Behavior Analysis:

    i.   Leverage user behavior insights from tools like heatmaps and recordings to inform optimization strategies.

14. Educational Opportunities:

a. Continuous Learning:

    i.   Encourage your team to participate in training programs, webinars, and conferences to stay current with industry best practices.

b. Certifications:

    i.   Invest in certifications for your team members to validate their expertise and knowledge.

15. Scenario Planning:

a. What-If Scenarios:

    i.   Develop what-if scenarios to anticipate potential challenges and plan preemptive strategies.

b. Risk Mitigation:

    i.   Establish risk mitigation plans for various scenarios to respond to unexpected challenges promptly.

16. Documentation and Knowledge Sharing:

a. Document Learnings:

    i.   Maintain comprehensive documentation of lessons learned, successful strategies, and areas for improvement.

b. Team Collaboration:

    i.   Foster collaboration and knowledge sharing within your team to ensure everyone benefits from collective insights.

Adapting to algorithm changes and industry trends requires a dynamic and informed approach. By staying proactive, continuously monitoring performance, and adjusting your strategies based on insights, your SEO efforts will be better positioned to withstand changes and contribute to long-term success.

FUTURE-PROOFING YOUR HVAC BUSINESS WITH SUSTAINABLE SEO PRACTICES

Future-proofing your HVAC business with sustainable SEO practices involves adopting strategies that align with current search engine algorithms and anticipate and adapt to future changes. Here's a guide to implementing sustainable SEO practices for long-term success:

1. User-Centric Content Creation:

a. Content Quality:

    i. Prioritize high-quality, informative content that addresses the needs and queries of your target audience.

b. Intent Alignment:

    i. Align content with user intent. Understand the search intent behind keywords and create content that fulfills those intents.

c. Diversification:

    i. Diversify content formats, including blog posts, videos, infographics, and interactive content.

2. Technical SEO Excellence:

a. Mobile Optimization:

    i. Ensure your website is mobile-friendly, as search engines increasingly prioritize mobile-first indexing.

b. Site Speed:

    i. Optimize page loading speed for a better user experience and improved search rankings.

c. Structured Data:

    i. Implement structured data to enhance search engines' visibility and understanding of your content.

3. Local SEO Emphasis:

a. Google My Business Optimization:

    i.   Optimize your Google My Business profile with accurate information, including business hours, services, and customer reviews.

b. Local Citations:

    i.   Consistently manage local citations across online directories to strengthen your local presence.

4. Quality Backlink Building:

a. Natural Link Building:

    i.   Focus on acquiring natural and high-quality backlinks through content partnerships, guest posting, and participation in industry events.

b. Link Diversity:

    i.   Build a diverse backlink profile from reputable sources within and outside the HVAC industry.

5. User Experience Enhancement:

a. Intuitive Navigation:

    i.   Design an intuitive and user-friendly website navigation structure.

b. Responsive Design:

    i.   Ensure your website is responsive and provides a seamless user experience across various devices.

6. Community Engagement:

a. Social Media Integration:

    i.   Integrate social media into your SEO strategy to enhance brand visibility and engagement.

b. Community Involvement:

    i.   Participate in local events, sponsorships, or community initiatives to strengthen your brand's local ties.

7. Continuous Monitoring and Analysis:

a. Regular Audits:

    i.   Conduct regular SEO audits to identify and address technical issues, content gaps, and opportunities for improvement.

b. Performance Metrics:

    i.   Monitor key performance metrics, such as organic traffic, keyword rankings, and conversion rates.

8. Adaptability to Algorithm Changes:

a. Stay Informed:

    i.   Stay updated on search engine algorithm changes and proactively adjust your strategies to align with new requirements.

b. Algorithm-Resilient Strategies:

    i.   Build resilience into your SEO approach by focusing on foundational practices that withstand algorithmic shifts.

9. Customer Feedback Integration:

a. Feedback Loops:

    i.   Establish customer feedback loops to understand their needs, concerns, and expectations.

b. Online Reviews:

    i.   Encourage and manage online reviews, addressing customer feedback promptly and transparently.

10. Educational Content and Thought Leadership:

a. Educational Resources:

   i.   Create informative and educational content that positions your HVAC business as an industry authority.

b. Thought Leadership:

   i.   Share insights, industry trends, and best practices to establish thought leadership in the HVAC space.

11. Strategic Keyword Planning:

a. Long-Tail Keywords:

   i.   Incorporate long-tail keywords that reflect specific HVAC services and address user queries.

b. Semantic SEO:

   i.   Embrace semantic SEO by understanding the context and relationships between keywords to enhance content relevance.

12. Innovation and Technology Adoption:

a. Embrace New Technologies:

   i.   Stay abreast of technological advancements and consider adopting innovative SEO tools and strategies.

b. Voice Search Optimization:

   i.   Prepare for the rise of voice search by optimizing content for natural language queries.

13. Scenario Planning and Risk Mitigation:

a. What-If Scenarios:

   i.   Develop scenarios for potential challenges, algorithm changes, or industry disruptions, and plan preemptive strategies.

b. Risk Mitigation Plans:

    i.   Have risk mitigation plans in place to address unforeseen challenges promptly.

14. Documentation and Knowledge Sharing:

a. Document Learnings:

    i.   Maintain a comprehensive documentation of successful strategies, lessons learned, and ongoing improvements.

b. Team Collaboration:

    i.   Foster collaboration and knowledge sharing within your SEO team to ensure collective insights benefit the organization.

15. Data-Driven Decision-Making:

a. Analytics Tools:

    i.   Utilize advanced analytics tools to gain insights into user behavior, preferences, and emerging trends.

b. Experimentation and Testing:

    i.   Conduct A/B testing and experiments to refine strategies and understand what resonates best with your audience.

Future-proofing your HVAC business with sustainable SEO practices involves a holistic approach that combines technical excellence, content quality, community engagement, and adaptability to industry changes. By embracing these practices, your HVAC business can build a resilient online presence that stands the test of time and industry evolution.

CONCLUSION

In conclusion, the success of an HVAC business in the digital age hinges on a robust and adaptive SEO strategy. From understanding the evolving landscape of consumer behavior to implementing a comprehensive A-Z SEO guide, this guide has explored the critical facets of leveraging search engine optimization to enhance online visibility, credibility, and customer engagement.

Key Takeaways:

1. **Digital Transformation:** The digital landscape has reshaped consumer behavior, emphasizing the need for HVAC businesses to establish a strong online presence.

2. **Importance of SEO:** SEO is instrumental in driving organic traffic, boosting brand visibility, and establishing credibility in a competitive market.

3. **Understanding Customer Behavior:** Knowledge of customer search patterns, decision-making processes, and expectations is crucial for tailoring SEO strategies effectively.

4. **A-Z SEO Guide for HVAC Dealers:** From keyword research and on-page optimization to off-page strategies, local SEO tactics, and analytics interpretation, the comprehensive A-Z guide covers the essential steps for HVAC businesses.

5.

6. **Results from Successful HVAC SEO Campaigns:** Case studies illustrate how implementing effective SEO practices can lead to tangible results, including increased organic traffic, higher rankings, and improved business performance.

7. **Measuring and Monitoring Success:** Key performance indicators (KPIs) and analytics tools are vital in measuring the effectiveness of SEO efforts and guiding ongoing optimization strategies.

8. **Adapting to Changes:** The dynamic nature of search engine algorithms and industry trends requires businesses to stay informed, be adaptable, and proactively adjust strategies to remain competitive.

9. **Future-Proofing with Sustainable Practices:** To future-proof an HVAC business, sustainable SEO practices should focus on user-centric content, technical excellence, local SEO emphasis, continuous monitoring, and adaptability to emerging technologies.

10. **Conclusion:** Success in the digital era demands a strategic and adaptive approach to SEO. HVAC businesses can build a resilient online presence and thrive in the competitive digital landscape by aligning SEO efforts with evolving consumer needs, staying abreast of industry trends, and maintaining a commitment to excellence.

As you embark on your SEO journey, remember that it's an ongoing process that requires dedication, continuous learning, and a commitment to delivering value to your audience. By embracing the principles outlined in this guide, your HVAC business can confidently navigate the digital landscape and set the stage for long-term success.

www.ingramcontent.com/pod-product-compliance
Lightning Source LLC
LaVergne TN
LVHW041205050326
832903LV00020B/469